JUST SAY NO

ROBERTA CAVA

Copyright © 2016 by Roberta Cava

All rights reserved. No part of this work covered by the copyrights hereon may be reproduced or used in any form or by any means - graphic, electronic or mechanical, including photocopying, recording, taping or information storage and retrieval systems - without the prior written permission of the publisher.

Just Say NO

Roberta Cava

Published by Cava Consulting

info@dealingwithdifficultpeople.info

Discover other titles by Roberta Cava at:
www.dealingwithdifficultpeople.info/books

National Library of Australia

Cataloguing-in-publication data:

ISBN 978-0-9944365-7-3

BOOKS BY ROBERTA CAVA

Non-Fiction

Dealing with Difficult People
(21 publishers – in 16 languages)
Dealing with Difficult Situations – at Work and at Home
Dealing with Difficult Spouses and Children
Dealing with Difficult Relatives and In-Laws
Dealing with Domestic Violence and Child Abuse
Dealing with School Bullying
Dealing with Workplace Bullying
Retirement Village Bullies
Just say NO
Keeping Our Children Safe
What am I going to do with the rest of my life?
Before tying the knot – Questions couples Must ask each other
Before they marry!
How Women can advance in business
Survival Skills for Supervisors and Managers
Human Resources at its Best!
Human Resources Policies and Procedures - Australia
Employee Handbook
Easy Come – Hard to go – The Art of Hiring, Disciplining and
Firing Employees
Time and Stress – Today's silent killers
Take Command of your Future – Make things Happen
Belly Laughs for All! – Volumes 1 to 4
Wisdom of the World! The happy, sad and wise things in life!

Fiction

That Something Special
Something Missing
Trilogy: Life Gets Complicated
Life Goes On
Life Gets Better

ACKNOWLEDGEMENTS

Many thanks to Doreen Orion, MD, *'I Know You Really Love Me;'* Lenore Walker, Karen Neilsen and Edmonton Area Inter-Agency Committee on Wife Assault Sources, *'Wife Assault - Hurts All of Us*;' Queensland University of Technology Survey; Elaine Hollingsworth, *'Smoke Gets in your Eyes;'* Raffi Cavoukian – *'Lightweb: Darkweb – Three reasons to reform social media before it reforms us;'* Sandra Dann, Working Women's Centre SA Inc.; TMP Worldwide; Morgan & Banks; NW Adelaide Heaqlth Service, Drake Personnel; Griffith University Wokrplace Bullying & Violence Project; Crime Stoppers Queensland – *'New synthetic drugs – real damage – doctor interview;'* and the Australia Drug Foundation 2014 for giving me permission to use their information.

Just Say NO
Table of Contents

Introduction

Chapter 1 – New Synthetic Drugs   *1*

What are the new synthetic drugs?
251 NBombe
Stopping synthetic drugs
Synthetic cannabis
How can harm from these drugs be reduced?
New idea for ensuring a party-goer's drugs are safe

Chapter 2 – Illicit Drugs   *9*

Use of drugs:
Alcohol
Analgesics
Benzodiazepines
Caffeine
Cannabis
Cocaine
Ecstacy
GHB
Hallucinogens
Heroin
Inhalants
Methamphetamine
Naloxone
Nitrous oxide
Oxycodone
Synthetic cannabis
Tobacco
Overdose
References
Crystal Methamphetamine (ICE)
Results of using ICE

Chapter 3 – Sex before marriage   29

Parent's responsibility
Date rape
Dating abuse
Adult rape victims
Dealing with stalkers

Chapter 4 – Pornography   39

The dangers of pornography
Distorted view of normal intimacy
Degradation of women
Parental role
Internet helps offenders

Chapter 5 – Domestic Violence   45

How safe is your relationship?
Has your partner ever?
Cycle of abuse:
- The tension-building phase
- The battering phase
- Remorse/contrite phase

Society's attitudes to domestic violence
Drug and alcohol abuse
What about women who use violence?
Mutual violence
Religion and domestic violence
Culture and domestic violence
Abusers believe:
Their victims believe:
Attitudes towards abuse
- Economic abuse
- Coercion and threats
- Emotional abuse
- Intimidating
- Using male privilege
- Using children

- Minimizing/denying abuse
- Isolating

Why do men abuse?
- The homoclyte
- The philanderer
- The competitor

Queensland University of Technology survey
How victims can be assisted

Chapter 6 – Child abuse　　　　　　　　　　　　　　69

How you can identify child abuse
What is child abuse
- Sexual
- Physical
- Tactile
- Existence
- Religious or cult
- Emotional neglect
- Emotional abuse
- Psychological
- Neglect/Physical neglect

Another form of abuse – smoking
Societal passivity to sexual abuse at home
Reporting abuse
The role of society
Domestic violence and children
Reactions of children exposed to domestic violence
Reactions of adolescents to domestic violence
- Behavioural problems

Chapter 7 – Elder Abuse　　　　　　　　　　　　　85

Barriers faced by elders
Vulnerability
Identifying abusers
What are the signs of elder abuse?

How can I tell if someone is being abusive?
- In long-term care setting

Elder self-neglect
If you know or suspect someone is being abused, you can:
How to obtain help in Australia

Chapter 8 - Social Media   93

The dangers of social media
Chat rooms
What is a paedophile?
How they interact with their targets
Female paedophiles
Church child abuse
Grooming the target
Contact rate of paedophiles
Other methods of communication
Internet safety
If you suspect your child is in trouble
Stranger danger
Addressing the disadvantages of social networking
Resources for parents and kids
Safety tips for using social media

Chapter 9 – School Bullying   109

Difference between child and adult bullying
Using fear
Case study
What constitutes school bullying
Dysfunctional home environment
How long does bullying affect the target?
Why are some children bullied
Profiles of bullies and targets
Four kinds of bullies
- Physical bullies
- Verbal bullies
- Relational bullies

- Reactive bullies

Sexual harassment

Types of pupil bullying behaviour:
- Physical aggression
- Damage to property
- Extortion
- Intimidation
- Abusive telephone, texts or e-mails
- Isolation
- Name calling
- Teasing

Effects of bullying
Why don't other students help the victim?
As parents
Is your child a bully?
Is your child a target?
Signs and symptoms of bullying behaviour
School hazing
Bullying of school personnel
Teacher behaviour
Preventing school bullying
Procedures for reporting bullying behaviour
Procedures for dealing with bullying behaviour
Program to deal with victims, bullies and their peers
Evaluation of school bullying policies
Selecting a school
- Presence of an anti-bullying policy

Recommendations

Chapter 10 – Cyber bullying   *143*

What is cyber bullying?
Who are the targets of cyber bullying?
What are the results to the target of bullying
The target's behaviour

The four stages of fear
Examples of bullying
How common is cyber bullying during the teen years?
Why do people cyber bully?
What can be done about cyber bullying?
Preventing cyber bullying
How to stop cyber bullying once it starts
Why is cyber bullying so serious?
Penalties for cyber bullying
Deal with cyber bullying when it happens
Why is cyber bullying so difficult to stop?
Can cyber bullying be stopped
When should the police be involved?
How to prevent your child from being targeted

Chapter 11 - Workplace bullying 161

The workplace epidemic
Cost to companies
New attitudes towards supervision
What do the experts have to say?
Lack of workplace bullying protection in Australia
Workplace stress management
Implementing an anti-bullying policy
Recommendations

Conclusion: 181

Web Connections: 183

INTRODUCTION

As we all go through life we're faced with making many tough decisions on what to do when faced with what could possibly be life-changing decisions. These decisions could be:

- how to say 'No' to using synthetic or illegal drugs like ICE (methamphetamine), heroin or cocaine.
- whether to have pre-marital sex;
- how to say 'No' to a persistent lover who wants sex;
- date rape and stalking;
- pornography;
- how to leave a domestic violence situation;
- how to report that an adult has mentally, physically or sexually abused a child;
- how a child can report being abused;
- how to deal with elder abuse;
- why social media is so dangerous;
- how to deal with school bullying;
- how to deal with cyber bullying:
- how to deal with workplace bullying;

Life is not easy, but many seem to make it through this minefield and live happy productive lives by 'Just saying NO.'

Chapter 1

SYNTHETIC DRUGS

An excellent video about the new synthetic drugs can be found on Youtube: *Crime Stoppers Queensland - New Synthetic Drugs: Real Damage - Doctor Interview*
https://www.youtube.com/watch?v=xp0_aWr77t4

What are Synthetic Drugs?

The term synthetic drugs is often used to describe drugs that are new to the market, or have become more widely used in recent years. The effect of these drugs mimics those of more established drugs like LSD, cocaine and cannabis but are sometimes much more potent.

The name 'synthetic drugs' can be confusing, because it doesn't distinguish these newer drugs from illicit drugs such as LSD, ecstasy and speed that are also synthesised from chemicals (rather than extracted from plants like cannabis, cocaine and heroin).

These new synthetic drugs can be ordered legally over the internet mainly from China where the drugs are legal. Producers of these substances have been traced back to factories in China that are selling them on the web. They're shipped by courier and seem to be able to slip under the radar of custom officials because of their packaging.

They're cheap and are sold as 'legal highs.' Locally, convenience stores, sex shops and tobacco shops were innocently selling the drugs, not knowing that they're causing horrific results. These 200+ drugs are now illegal in Australia.

There have been many deaths and users (some of them very young) suffer from terrible health problems such as strokes, heart damage, kidney/renal damage where some have had to go on dialysis. Imagine a fourteen-year-old having a stroke or heart attack?

Others have violent outbursts, psychosis, irrational fears and depression. Some become so depressed that they commit suicide because they get in trouble at school, steal from their parents and others, commit crimes and can be shunned by their former friends who do not use drugs. Others have had to drop out of school because they can't think straight.

Over two hundred of these new synthetic drugs are being sold and as one is banned, another one appears with a slightly different chemical makeup.

Some are marketed in little packets that resemble collector cards of sports legends and many parents don't know that they're dangerous synthetic drugs.

These synthetic drugs can be packaged as party pills, powders, herbal highs, bath salts, teas or even plant food, but often contain new, but untested chemicals designed to mimic the effects of drugs like cannabis, LSD and amphetamines.

They have names such as: OMG, Tai High, Kryp2nite, Rave, Blueberry, Smacked, Kapow, Amsterdam Royal, K2, Black Mamba, Spice, Benzo Fury, Kronic, Minga and White Revolver.

251 NBombe:

The one that has caused innumerable deaths – ***251-NBome (i.e.: N-Bomb) is twenty-five times stronger than LSD.*** It only takes a milligram of this drug to kill – the size of several grains of sand.

In October, 2016, twenty-one people were taken to Gold Coast Queensland hospitals when they ingested this drug and 27-year-old Rikki Stephens (a Victorian football player) died on October 20th.

251 NBombe drugs are hallucinogens – that is, drugs that distort perceptions – and can cause psychosis (a loss of contact with reality) in certain people. Others aren't even aware they're taking NBOMe because they think they're buying LSD. The only way users can tell they haven't bought LSD is by the taste. LSD is tasteless – 251NBombe tastes bitter. So, if anyone has discovered their LSD tastes bitter – they need to immediately obtain medical help.

Stopping synthetic drugs:

When one substance in Australia is banned, the legal process takes so long that there's plenty of time for another drug to take its place. The Ministry of Health have estimated that $140 million of these drugs were sold over just 10 months.

These synthetic drugs can have other toxic effects on the body not experienced with LSD including: seizures, agitation, heart and blood vessel problems, hypothermia, metabolic acidosis (the kidneys can't remove enough acid from the body) organ failure and even death.

One teenager took one of these drugs, began talking a mile a minute, running around in circles, had a terrible panic attack and jumped off a balcony to his death. His friend wandered over a busy roadway and was hit by a car.

Synthetic cannabis:

Another drug that's deadly is the synthetic cannabis that is *one hundred times stronger than marijuana*. Synthetic cannabis is essentially plant material that has been sprayed with chemicals and can cause irreparable kidney damage.

People smoke these products so they can experience a 'high,' similar to marijuana. It's been associated with an increasing number of deaths and serious adverse effects when taken by naïve users.

Some people have also experienced severe mental health effects including hallucinations, psychosis, panic and anxiety after taking synthetic cannabis. Although they're popular among young people (especially teenagers) evidence suggests they are also popular with adults in their twenties and thirties. A 2011 survey of 316 users of synthetic cannabis products found that fifty per cent of users were aged twenty-eight and over and a quarter were over thirty-five.

The synthetic drug trade has invaded our youth and we're having a terrible time keeping these drug dealers from hurting our youngsters. Some of the people selling these synthetic drugs are earning up to thirty thousand dollars a day, so it's hard to discourage them from selling them when the profits are so good. There's a new counterculture that exploits the legal loopholes that give users a mind-altering high by changing the chemical makeup of synthetic drugs to keep ahead of what the police can do to stop them.

Spice was the earliest in a series of synthetic cannabis products sold in many European countries. Since then several similar products have been developed, such as Kronic, Northern Lights, Mojo, Lightning Gold, Lightning Red and Godfather.

The Australian government has imposed a blanket ban on possession or selling substances like alcohol, tobacco and food that have substantially the same effect as a dangerous drug. However, for years, stores throughout Australia were openly selling illicit psycho-active drugs which mimic marijuana, cocaine, LSD and ecstasy. Some of these drugs have up to one hundred times the active ingredient in illicit drugs such as cannabis, making users guinea pigs and crash-test dummies, while the criminals rake in the profits.

Sex shop owners and tobacco shops were the main suppliers, but now most of these drugs are ordered on-line directly from China. The Chinese drug dealers often send them to other countries before they are delivered to their clients throughout the world.

Synthetic cannabis is sold as a tea for eighty dollars for a three-gram packet. These special teas are dipped in a potentially fatal hallucinogenic substance that has led directly to the deaths of many.

On one occasion, four twenty-year-olds went to a 'bucks' party. None had taken drugs before, but were convinced by a 'friend' (some friend) to try marihuana. They agreed, not knowing that the drug was not marihuana, but the new synthetic cannabis. Within two days, two were dead, one was on dialysis and the other had lost most of his brain cells.

Our biggest problem is that we don't know what's in many of these drugs – but we do know the results – organ failure, seizures, paranoia and sometimes death.

Community-minded people are encouraged to report seeing any of these drugs before someone else ends up in an emergency ward of a hospital or die.

At the end of May, 2015 a drug derived from cannabis lost its status as a poison in Australia and will be included on the list of prescription-only medications that can be used for relieving epileptic seizures and several other medical ailments. Trials of medicinal cannabis began in 2015 in Queensland, NSW and Victoria. Cannabis itself remains illegal in all states of Australia.

How can harm from these drugs be reduced?

Be aware of the following (some of this advice comes from the Australian Drug Foundation):

Note: EPS is short for 'emerging psychoactive substances.' (The term psychoactive means the drugs affect the brain causing changes in thought, mood and/or behaviour).

Because products are constantly changing, it's very hard to determine the effects of EPS, even if the person has taken them before. So activities like driving, swimming and operating machinery are especially unsafe for anyone using these drugs.

Many EPS contain a range of fillers and numbing agents that could lead to health problems, particularly if injected.

Some products can cause seizures and/or fast or irregular heartbeats. These are especially problematic if the user has any underlying health conditions.

Given the large number of these drugs on the market, it can be difficult for medical practitioners to know how to treat someone who has overdosed on or has health problems caused by EPS. Treatment could be quicker and more effective if someone could advise exactly what has been taken and the dosage. Supplying the packet might be helpful.

If someone is badly affected by any drug, call an ambulance immediately.

Don't let fear of police involvement affect your decision.

Waiting a few hours can make the difference between someone being saved or being dead.

Ambulance officers will not call on police to be involved unless there's a death, serious violence where they need help controlling the situation, or if the person has illicit drugs on them when they arrive at a hospital.

New idea for ensuring a party-goer's drugs are safe:

Two countries are tackling the drug situation in a unique way – and other countries are seriously looking at it because it seems to be working. Establishments where they know the patrons are using drugs – are setting up a pill analysis to tell the owner whether the drug is safe to take. The person remains anonymous – but is given a number when they leave their pills with the tester.

Half an hour later the drug user returns to the testing site and is informed whether the drug is safe. If the drug is too potent for the weight of the user, the testers will suggest that the owner take one quarter or one-half of the pill rather than a full pill that could have dangerous after-effects. For some pills, the owner is advised that there are dangerous chemicals in the pills and they should not take them. The owner of the drugs leaves the testing area with his/her drugs.

In Austria and The Netherlands experts are running these drug-checking services. Studies of Austria's program (which has run for over two decades) show that one-third of the people who had their drugs tested, decided not to take them; proving that drug-checking services reduced drug use - rather than increased it.

There's a big difference in the way people use ecstasy in Australia compared to Europe and often they don't have an idea of the real contents of what they're taking. That lack of knowledge, combined with Australia's position as the largest per-capita users of ecstasy in the world, is a recipe for disaster. This drug testing might be the answer.

However, NSW Drugs Squad Commander Tony Cooke explained that he doesn't think drug-checking will ever be allowed in Australia because that would be a 'tacit support' of drug use, and 'these drugs are illegal.'

Many would think that this new concept will only encourage drug use, but banning the drugs doesn't seem to be working and some think it's an alternative to seizing the drugs, arresting and jailing the users (who will leave jail and continue buying more drugs).

Conclusion:

Before taking any synthetic drug, understand that for your own safety you need to 'Just say NO.'

Chapter 11
ILLICIT DRUGS

Use of drugs:

© *Australian Drug Foundation 2014.* Used with permission - See more at: www.adf.org.au/legal-miscellaneous/australian-drug-foundation-copyright-requests#sthashZAdBXstZ.dpuf

Alcohol:

National:

- Alcohol is the most widely used drug in Australia.
- 86.2% of Australians aged fourteen years and over have drunk alcohol one or more times in their lives[1].
- 37.3% of Australians aged fourteen years and over consume alcohol on a weekly basis[1].
- The age group with the greatest number of Australians who drink daily *is seventy plus years*[1].
- Around one in five (18.2%) Australians over fourteen drink at levels that put them at risk of alcohol-related harm over their lifetime[1].
- Around one in six (15.6%) people aged twelve years or older had consumed eleven or more standard drinks on a single drinking occasion in the past twelve months[1].
- One in four women drink alcohol while pregnant, even though the Australian Alcohol Guidelines recommend not drinking during this time[1].
- $7B is generated by alcohol-related tax. But alcohol costs society $15.3b annually[3].
- Alcohol caused more than twice as many deaths (3,494) than road accidents (1,600) in 2005[4].

- One in ten workers say they have experienced the negative effects of a co-worker's use of alcohol[5,6].

Young People:
- Young Australians (aged fourteen to twenty-four) have their first full serve of alcohol at 15.7 years on average[1].
- 72.3% of twelve to seventeen year olds have not consumed alcohol in the last twelve months[1].
- 17% of fifteen to eighteen years old say they had sex when drunk which they later regretted[7].
- Alcohol contributes to the three major causes of teen death: injury, homicide and suicide[8].
- Friends or acquaintances are the most likely sources of alcohol for twelve to seventeen year olds (45.4%), with parents being the second most likely source (29.3%)[1].

Victoria:

On average, there were thirty alcohol-related ambulance attendances in metropolitan Melbourne per day in 2012/13 (25% increase from 2011/12), and ten per day in regional Victoria (30% increase). The average age of these patients was forty years[10].

Alcohol was the reason for most drug-related ambulance attendances, with 11,159 attendances in 2012/13 compared to 3,159 for benzodiazepines, 1,901 for heroin, 1,584 for non-opioid analgesics (such as paracetamol) and 1,112 for crystal methamphetamine (ICE)[10].

Analgesics:

National:

- 7.7% of Australians aged fourteen years and older have used analgesics for non-medical purposes one or more times in their life[1].

- 3.3% of Australians aged fourteen years and over have used analgesics for non-medical purposes in the previous twelve months[1].

Young People:

Young Australians (aged fourteen to twenty-four) first try analgesics for non-medical purposes at fifteen years on average[1].

Analgesics are the most commonly used drug (licit or illicit) among twelve- to seventeen-year-olds. By the age of thirteen, 95% of this age group have used analgesics (mostly for headaches and/or cold and flu symptoms)[9].

4% of twelve to seventeen year olds take analgesics from home without permission and 3% buy them[9].

Victoria:

The number of opioid analgesic ambulance attendances in 2012/13 increased significantly compared with the previous year – 55% increase in metropolitan Melbourne and 21% in regional Victoria. There was also an increase for non-opioid analgesics – 38% in metropolitan Melbourne and 34% in regional Victoria[10].

Non-opioid analgesics (such as paracetamol) are the third most common drug involved in ambulance attendances, following alcohol and benziodiazepines[10].

Benzodiazepines

National:

- 4.5% of Australians aged fourteen years and over have used tranquillisers/sleeping pills (including benzodiazepines) for non-medical purposes one or more times in their life[1].
- 1.6% of Australians aged fourteen years and over have used tranquillisers (including benzodiazepines) for non-medical purposes in the previous twelve months[1].

Young people:

Young Australians (aged fourteen to twenty-four) first try tranquilisers for non-medical purposes at 18.2 years on average[1].

Victoria:

Benzodiazepines contributed to fifty-six deaths in Victoria in 2010, representing almost 17% of the total number of drug-related deaths investigated by the Coroners Court of Victoria in that year[11].

In 2012/13 there was an average of eight ambulances attendances per day for benzodiazepines in metropolitan Melbourne, and two per day in regional Victoria. Both represent small increases from the previous year. The average age of the patients involved in these attendances was thirty-eight to forty years[10].

Benzodiazepines are the second most common drug involved in ambulance attendances in Victoria, after alcohol[10].

Betel nut:

Around 10–20% of the world's population chews betel nut in some form. This makes it the fourth most widely-used psychoactive substance, after nicotine, alcohol and caffeine[12,13].

Caffeine: (including energy drinks)

In Australia between 2004 and 2010, there were 297 calls to the NSW Poisons Information Line concerning toxicity from caffeinated energy drinks. The most commonly reported symptoms included palpitations, tachycardia, tremors, shaking, agitation and restlessness.[27]

Consumption:

One billion cups of coffee per year were consumed at cafés, restaurants and other outlets in Australia in 2006[26].

Consumption of coffee has doubled over the past thirty years from 1.2 to 2.4 kg per person in Australia[26].

Global coffee consumption increased in 2010, with consumers spending a total of $10.7 billion, which is equivalent to 2.4 kilograms of coffee per person, per year[28].

Sales of energy drinks in Australia and New Zealand increased from 34.5 million litres in 2001 to 155.6 litres in 2010[29].

Cocaine:

National:

- 8.1% of Australians aged fourteen years and over have used cocaine one or more times in their life[1].
- 2.1% of Australians aged fourteen years and over have used cocaine in the previous 12 months[1].

Young people:

- Young Australians (aged fourteen to twenty-four) first try cocaine at 19.2 years on average[1].
- The 1.7% of twelve to seventeen year olds who take cocaine have only used it once or twice[9].

Cannabis:

National:

- 34.8% of Australians aged fourteen years and over have used cannabis one or more times in their life[1].
- 10.2% of Australians aged fourteen years and over have used cannabis in the previous twelve months[1].

Young people:

- Young Australians (aged fourteen to twenty-four) first try cannabis at 16.7 years on average[1].
- 14.8% of twelve to seventeen year olds have tried cannabis – it is the most commonly used illicit drug among this age group[9].

Victoria:

There were 3.88 cannabis-related ambulance attendances in metropolitan Melbourne per day and 1.52 in regional Victoria in 2012/13. The average age of the patients involved in these attendances was thirty years[10].

Between 2011/12 and 2012/13, there was a 10% increase in the number of attendances for cannabis in metropolitan and regional Victoria that resulted in hospital transportation[10].

Ambulance attendances for cannabis continue to rise, with more than double in 2012/13 than in 2003/04 in metropolitan Melbourne[10].

Ecstasy:

National:

- 10.9% of Australians aged fourteen years and over have used ecstasy one or more times in their life[1].
- 2.5% of Australians aged fourteen years and over have used ecstasy in the previous 12 months[1].

Young people:

- Young Australians (aged fourteen to twenty-four) first try ecstasy at 18.2 years on average[1].
- 2.7% of twelve- to seventeen-year-olds have tried ecstasy[9].

Victoria:

In both metropolitan and regional Victoria, there was an over 60% increase in the number of ambulance attendances where the patient believed they had taken ecstasy between 2011/12 and 2012/13[10].

The proportion of attendances where the patient reported having ecstasy and alcohol decreased by 10% in metropolitan Melbourne[10].

The number of attendances resulting in hospital transportation increased in 2012/13, which could indicate an increase in harmful substances being included in ecstasy pills[10].

GHB:

[GHB (gamma hydroxybutyrate) is a depressant drug that slows down the messages travelling between the brain and body. Other names G, fantasy, grievous bodily harm (GBH), liquid ecstasy, liquid E, liquid X, Georgia Home Boy, soap, scoop, cherry meth, blue nitro. GHB is usually swallowed, but sometimes it's injected or inserted anally.]

National:
- 0.9% of Australians aged fourteen years and over have used GHB one or more times in their life[1].

Young people:
- Young Australians (aged fourteen to twenty-four) first try GHB at 20.1 years on average[1].

Victoria:

The number of GHB ambulance attendances in 2012/13 increased by 42% (up to 578 attendances) in metropolitan Melbourne and 3% (42) in regional Victoria from the previous year[10].

[Author's note re: Date Rape Drugs:

The most common date rape drugs - also called club drugs, are flunitrazepam (Rohypnol), also called roofies; gamma hydroxybutyric acid (GHB), also called liquid ecstasy, ketamine, blue nitro, scoop, fantasy or Special K. These drugs may come as pills, liquids, or powders.

Alcohol may also be considered a date rape drug because it affects judgment and behaviour and can be used to help commit sexual assault.

The club drug 'ecstasy' (MDMA) has also been used to commit sexual assault.

Young girls and women need to protect themselves by not accepting drinks from others, not sharing drinks, watching their drinks, and having a non-drinking friend with them to make sure they're not secetly given one of these drugs.

If you suspect you or (another party-goer) has been exposed to a date rape drug, call your local emergency number and have a safe person drive you (or them) to a hospital emergency room immediately. If they or you have been sexually assaulted after being given a drug, do not have a shower or change your clothing and get to a hospital emergency room immediately where date-rape tests will be conducted.]

Hallucinogens:

National:

- 9.4% of Australians aged fourteen years and over have used hallucinogens one or more times in their life[1].
- 1.3% of Australians aged fourteen years and over have used hallucinogens in the previous twelve months[1].

Young people:

- Young Australians (aged fourteen to twenty-four) first try hallucinogens at 18.5 years on average[1].
- 3% of twelve to seventeen year olds have tried hallucinogens such as LSD[9].

Inhalants:

National:

- 3.8% of Australians aged fourteen years and over have used inhalants one or more times in their life[1].
- 0.8% of Australians aged fourteen years and over have used inhalants in the previous twelve months[1].

Young people:

- Young Australians (aged fourteen to twenty-four) first try inhalants at 16.9 years of age on average[1].
- Around one in five twelve to seventeen-year-olds have deliberately sniffed inhalants at least once[9].

Victoria:

In 2012/13 the number of ambulance attendances related to inhalant use in metropolitan Melbourne dropped by 10% - from 135 in 2011/12 to 122 in 2012/13. Attendances in regional Victoria increased by 121% - from fourteen to thirty-five years of age[10].

Heroin:

National:

- 1.2% of Australians aged fourteen years and older have used heroin one or more times in their life[1].
- 0.1% of Australians aged fourteen years of age and older have used heroin in the previous twelve months[1].

Young people:

- Young Australians (aged fourteen- to twenty-four-years-of-age) first try heroin at 16.9 years on average[1].
- 1.6% of twelve- to seventeen-year-olds have tried heroin[9].

Victoria:

There were 5.21 ambulance attendances related to heroin in metropolitan Melbourne and 0.28 in regional Victoria per day in 2012/13 (these numbers include non-fatal overdose)[10].

There was a 13% decrease in the number of ambulance attendances for heroin overdose in metropolitan Melbourne and 15% decrease in regional Victoria in 2012/13 compared to the previous year[10].

Naloxone:

Naloxone successfully reversed twenty-three opioid overdoses between 2011 and 2013, during a peer administration trial in Canberra[14].

In Australia in 2009, there were 563 accidental deaths attributed to opioids among people aged 15-54 years. In the over fifty-five age group, there were seventy deaths. Many of these deaths were due to multiple drugs being taken including prescription opioids[15].

Methamphetamine: (including ice)

National:

- 7.0% of Australians aged fourteen years of age and over have used methamphetamines one or more times in their life.[1]
- 2.1% of Australians aged fourteen-years-of-age and over have used methamphetamines in the previous twelve months. Of these people, 50.4% report crystal or ice as main form of the drug used.[1]

Young people:

- Young Australians (aged fourteen to twenty-four) first try meth/amphetamines at 18.6 years on average[1].
- 2.9% of twelve to seventeen-year-olds have tried amphetamines[9].

Victoria:

The daily number of all amphetamine-related ambulance attendances in 2012/13 increased significantly compared with the previous year – 88% increase in metropolitan Melbourne and a 198% in regional Victoria. This is attributed to an increase in the number of attendances relating to crystal meth-amphetamine (ICE).[10]

In metropolitan Melbourne, there was an 88% increase in the number of attendances for ICE (crystal methamphetamine) between 2011/12 and 2012/13, up to an average of three per day. In regional Victoria, the increase was 198%, up to 0.63 per day[10].

ICE (crystal methamphetamine) is the fourth most common drug involved in ambulance attendances, following alcohol, benzodiazepines and non-opioid analgesics (such as paracetamol)[10].

New psychoactive substances:

New psychoactive substances (NPS) are being developed at an unprecedented rate. The European Monitoring Centre for Drugs and Drug Addiction (EMCDDA) and Europol currently monitors more than 450 NPS, which is close to double the number of substances controlled under the United Nations international drug control conventions. More than half of these have been reported in the last three years [16].

National:

- 0.4% of Australians aged fourteen years and over have used new psychoactive substances at some stage in their lives[1].
- 0.4% of Australians aged fourteen years and over have used new psychoactive substances in the previous twelve months[1].

United Kingdom:

In the UK, there has been an increasing trend in NPS deaths with sharp increases between 2011 and 2012 (twenty-nine to fifty-two deaths). The number of deaths involving NPS rose again in 2013 by 15% to sixty deaths[17].

Nitrous Oxide:

According to the Australian Trends in Ecstasy and Related Drug Markets 2013 Survey one quarter (25%) of the sample reported recent nitrous oxide use in the six months preceding the survey. This is comparable with 2012 results. Use was highest in Victoria (45%)[31].

Oxycodone:

National:

- The amount of oxycodone being prescribed by doctors increased from 95.1 kg in 1999 to 1270.7 kg in 2008 – a thirteen-fold increase[18].

Victoria:

The amount of oxycodone being prescribed by doctors increased nine-fold from 7.5 mg per capita in 2000 to 67.5 mg per capita in 2009[18].

Pharmacotherapy drugs:

(methadone, buprenorphine and naloxone)

On a snapshot day in June 2012, 46,697 clients were receiving pharmacotherapy treatment in Australia. 68% received methadone, 19% received buprenorphine–naloxone and 13% received buprenorphine.[23]

Synthetic cannabis:

An on-line study recently conducted in 2012 found that of the people who use the drug:

- The median age is 27 years;
- 70% are male;
- 78% are employed;
- 7% use daily;[20]

National:

- 1.3% of Australians aged fourteen years and over have used synthetic cannabis at some stage in their lives[1].
- 1.2% of Australians aged fourteen years and over have used synthetic cannabis in the previous twelve months[1].
- According to Australian data from the Global Drug Survey, synthetic cannabis was the twentieth most commonly used drug – 4.1% of respondents had used this type of drug in the last twelve months[20].

Tobacco:

National:

- 39.8% of Australians aged fourteen years and over have used tobacco[1].
- More males than females are daily smokers across all age groups[1].
- People who smoke aged twelve years and over smoked on average 95.9 cigarettes per week[1].
- Around one in eight (12.8%) Australians aged fourteen years and over smoke daily[1].
- In 2012, 12.5% of all mothers reported that they had smoked while pregnant. This is down from 13.2% in 2011 and 13.5% in 2010[30].
- Teenage mothers accounted for 10.2% of all mothers who reported smoking during pregnancy. But of all teenage mothers, 34.9% reported smoking[30].

Young people:

- Young Australians (aged fourteen-to twenty-four) have their first full cigarette at 15.9 years on average[1].
- 77% of twelve- to seventeen-year-olds have not smoked. The proportion of twelve- to seventeen-year-olds who

have never smoked decreases in the older age groups, but by age seventeen more than half have still never smoked[9].

- Around 4% of all twelve- to seventeen-year-olds have smoked more than one hundred cigarettes in their lifetime, which peaks at 9% among seventeen-year-olds[9].

Overdose:

In Australia in 2009, there were 563 accidental deaths attributed to opioids among people aged fifteen to fifty-four years. In the over fifty-five age group, there were seventy deaths. Many of these deaths were due to multiple drugs being taken including prescription opioids. Alcohol and other drug experts suggest that opioid-related deaths in Australia are increasing.[21]

Of all illegal substances, heroin and other opioids were involved with the largest number of drug-related deaths, despite the number of people using them being low compared to other substances. Amphetamines including 'ice' have the second highest death rate of illegal drugs.[22]

References:

1. Australian Institute of Health and Welfare. (2014). Canberra: AIHW.
2. Callinan, S., & Room, R. (2012). *Alcohol consumption during pregnancy: results from the 2010 National Drug Strategy Household Survey*. Canberra: Foundation for Alcohol Research and Education.
3. Manning, M., Smith, C., & Mazerolle, P. (2013). *The societal costs of alcohol misuse in Australia*. Canberra: Australian Institute of Criminology.
4. Collins, D., & Lapsley, H. (2008). *The costs of tobacco, alcohol and illicit drug abuse to Australian society in 2004/05*. Canberra: Commonwealth of Australia.

5. Laslett, A.M., Catalano, P., Chikritzhs, T., et al. (2010). *The range and magnitude of alcohol's harm to others*. Fitzroy: AER Centre for Alcohol Policy Research.
6. Dale, C.E., & Livingston, M. (2010). The burden of alcohol drinking on co-workers in the Australian workplace. *Medical Journal of Australia, 193*(3), 138-140.
7. Smith, A., Agius, P., Mitchell, A., Barrett, C., & Pitts, M. (2009). *Secondary students and sexual health 2008: Results of the 4th National Survey of Australian Secondary Students, HIV/AIDS and Sexual Health*. Melbourne: Australian Research Centre in Sex, Health and Society.
8. National Health and Medical Research Council. (2009). *Australian guidelines to reduce health risks from drinking alcohol*, Canberra: NHMRC.
9. White, V., & Bariola, E. (2012). *Australian secondary school students' use of tobacco, alcohol, and over-the-counter and illicit substances in 2011*. Melbourne: The Cancer Council, Victoria.
10. Lloyd, B., Matthews, S., & Gao, C.X. (2014). *Ambo Project – Alcohol and drug related ambulance attendances: Trends in alcohol and drug related ambulance attendances in Victoria 2012/13*. Fitzroy: Turning Point Alcohol and Drug Centre.
11. Coroners Court of Victoria. (2012). *Finding into death with inquest, Inquest in the Death of David Andrew Trengrove*, Delivered on 18 May 2012.
12. World Health Organization. (2012). Geneva: World Health Organization.
13. Ashock, L., Deepika, N., Sujatha, G.P., & Shiva P.S. (2011). 'Areca nut: To chew or not to chew?'. *e-Journal of Dentistry, 1*(3), 46–50.
14. Olsen, A., McDonald, D., Lenton, S., & Dietze P. (2014). Canberra: ACT Health.

15. Roxburgh, A., & Burns, L. (2013). Sydney: National Drug and Alcohol Research Centre (NDARC).
16. European Monitoring Centre for Drugs and Drug Addiction (EMCDDA). (2015). New psychoactive substances in Europe – An update from the EU Early Warning System, Lisbon: EMCDDA. .
17. Office for National Statistics. (2014). 2013 Newport: Office for National Statistics.
18. Rintoul, A.C., Dobbin, M., Drummer, O.H., & Ozanne-Smith, J. (2011). Increasing deaths involving oxycodone, Victoria, Australia, 2000-09. *Injury Prevention, 17*(4), 254–259.
19. Barratt, M.J. (2012)., Melbourne: Yarra Drug and Health Forum.
20. Global Drug Survey. (2014). London: Global Drug Survey.
21. Roxburgh, A., & Burns, L. (2013). Sydney: National Drug and Alcohol Research Centre (NDARC).

[Author's note: In 2013 the number of Australians being treated for codeine addiction had tripled to more than 1,000 a year, up from 318 in 2003. An intake of eighty tablets a day can cause significant damage to organs. In 2010, a spike in people abusing the painkillers sparked a supply change where products such as Nurofen Plus, Panadeine and Panadeine Extra were sold in smaller packs and issued by pharmacists.

The most used drug in the 1960s was diazepam but was available only from the person's GP.]

Crystal Methamphetamine (ICE):

Crystal methamphetamine (ICE) use in Australia is almost eight times the US level and almost five times the UK Level. Users spend an average of $300 to $500 per day feeding their habit and two-thirds admitted they committed crime to pay for

Just Say NO

it. Young people are turning to ICE as a cheaper alternative to alcohol.

ICE lasts longer than LSD, cocaine, ecstasy and speed. A single hit floods the brain with dopamine making the person feel elated, alert and focused. However, the regular and huge bursts of dopamine that at first made the person feel great, wears out the pleasure-producing regions of their brain and they begin to feel depressed and agitated at the same time.

Many become hooked on ICE because of the terrible 'downers' they have as they come off the 'high.' This keeps them using again and again until they simply can't get off the drug. Only professional rehabilitation can get them through the trauma of stopping the use of this drug.

'Meth Mouth' has cost Australians $1 million plus for prisoner's dental work in the past year. Stimulants such as methamphetamine cause 23% of those costs resulting in stained or rotting teeth. People in their 20s are losing all their teeth.

Here are some examples of the devastating results of using Ice:

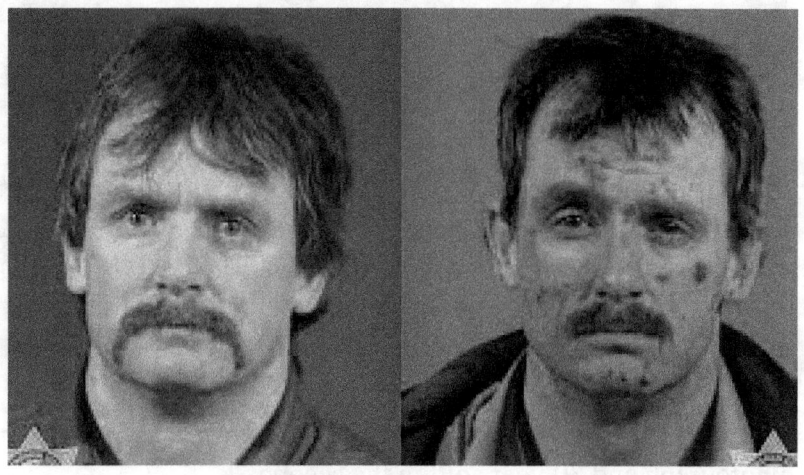

Not only do they appear to have the worst case of acne you've ever seen, but when they smile, you will note that their teeth are badly discoloured and are rotting away.

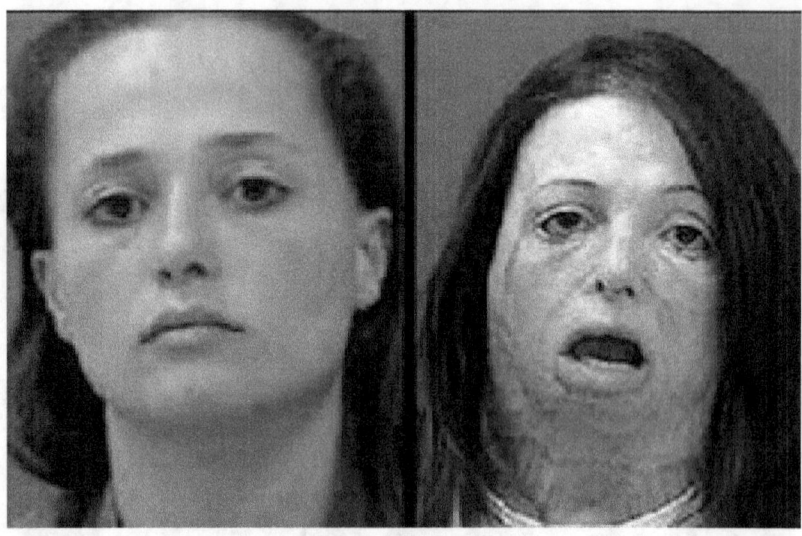

The woman in this set of pictures was 27 years old in the first photograph and 30 years old in the second.

Heather Raybon was left permanently scarred with terrible facial burns after being caught in a blast at a meth lab in 2004. Police in Florida said that despite the life-changing incident, the 31-year-old has continued to try to manufacture crystal meth. She has undergone numerous facial surgeries in the past seven years.

The third picture shows how she looked several years later.

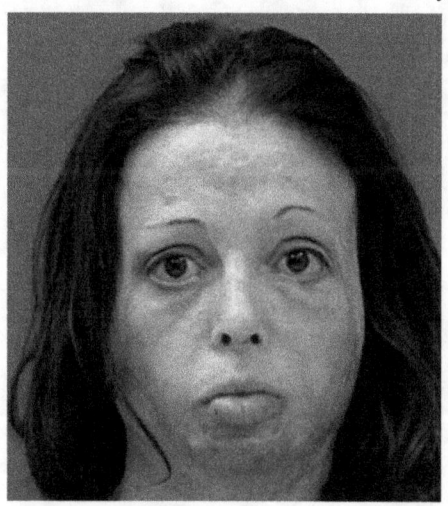

ICE users now account for nine out of ten people seeking help from some drug services. ICE addicts usually lose weight because they may not sleep or eat – just smoke ICE with a glass pipe day and night. They lose teeth and their bodies become covered with drug sores.

ICE is a stimulant drug, which means it speeds up the messages travelling between the brain and the body. It's a type of methamphetamine, which is generally stronger, more addictive and has more harmful side effects than the powder form known as speed.

In Australia one 14-year-old ICE-addicted girl living in Brisbane costs the state $12,000 a week for her care, because she refuses to stop using ICE and keeps running away to earn money to buy more drugs.

Former NSW premier Neville Wran's daughter Harriet Wran was arrested on August 13, 2014 accused of murdering a drug dealer. She battled an addiction to ICE before her arrest.

Conclusion:

Like with the other situations discussed in this book – 'Just say NO' when asked or are tempted to take illicit drugs.

Chapter 3

SEX BEFORE MARRIAGE

Parent's responsibility:

Parents are advised to educate their children at an early age to respect their own and bodies of each other. At an early age they would discuss 'stranger danger' and what to do if a situation like that happened.

Prior to their children's puberty, they would discuss what sex is all about and how to say 'No' if they don't want it. They would especially speak to their sons to advise that they could be charged with rape if the woman objects to having sex or is a female under the age of 16.

Parents would discuss sexual protection and describe what normal sex is all about and thoroughly discourage the watching of pornography.

Unfortunately if one puts the word pornography into Google, it's usually hard porn that pops up and can give children a distorted view of what the sex act, intimacy and closeness is all about. We will be discussing this in the next chapter.

Date Rape:

One study presented at the American Psychological Association suggest that 28 per cent of dating relationships contain some kind of physical, emotional or sexual abuse against women. The Stockholm Syndrome might be even more likely to develop in young women's dating relationships. One reason is that young women are more likely to perceive violence as signs of love. Young men in dating relationships tend to receive a lot of peer support for exhibiting behaviour that's masculine, aggressive and meant to control women.

- One in ten high school students have experienced some form of abuse in their dating relationships.

- One in eight women living with a male partner experiences some kind of abuse.
- At some time during their lives, one in four females and one in three males have been victims of unwanted sexual acts.

Dating abuse

Usually when we think of abuse and assault (battering) we think of it in physical terms - being hit, kicked, punched or maybe 'just' slapped around:

'He never really hit me, he just used to push me against the wall and he only pushed me down once.'

Not all abuse is physical. There are kinds that leave no marks. They are psychological and emotional abuse. This kind of abuse can take many forms, from being put down in little ways, being told that you're ugly, fat or stupid, to being bugged and harassed into doing something that you may not have wanted TO DO. This kind of abuse usually happens when you are isolated or when you don't spend time with other friends or family. It's important to have somebody to talk to - as a reality check - when you're being told this about yourself. It's so much harder to recognise and talk about this kind of abuse, because there are no visible signs.

> *'He thought my friends were too young, so we always partied and hung around with his friends. The first time we broke up, I noticed none of my friends were left.'*

Boyfriends who do or say these kinds of things are trying to control you and keep you from being independent. Remember that neither they nor anybody else has that right.

Another kind of abuse is forced sexual contact or intimacy. Sometimes you might start a sexual relationship with your boyfriend because you think that you might lose him if you didn't. It can mean being cajoled and pleaded with - so you feel guilty - to being actually forced. It's your right to decide when and how you want sex. When your boyfriend ignores this, it amounts to harassment, physical assault and rape. It's your right to say 'NO' and mean it.

'I said I didn't want to fool around. He called me a tease.'

'It seemed like he didn't listen when I told him I didn't like it.'

'I gave in. I didn't want to fight about it any more.'

'I thought that if I didn't go along, he wouldn't love me any more.'

There are many reasons why you might not walk away from a relationship. There's a lot of social pressure to have a boyfriend to take you to parties or just to go out with. If you don't have a boyfriend, people sometimes think there's something wrong with you or sometimes even see you as threatening; that you're 'not okay.' Sometimes staying with a boyfriend who batters you is less frightening than being alone in a society that measures your worth by whether you have a partner or not.

'Everybody thinks he's such a hunk, they don't know what he's really like.'

'Whenever I cried, he'd always tell me he could go out with any other girl and I'd better shut up or he would. I believed him.'

'He was so jealous about everybody that I looked at. For a long time, I thought that it meant he loved me.'

A woman who is lonely or isolated is more susceptible to battering, because she has no one to talk to. Many become isolated from their family support system because the boyfriend doesn't like them. She eventually can feel that her boyfriend is the only one that loves and cares about her. This makes his behaviour even more confusing and she may start to feel that she deserves what he's doing to her. Her self-esteem slowly deteriorates to the point where he has a great deal of power over her and she may start to believe that she deserve the battering. Nobody does!

Many women feel that it is their fault the relationship is not working because their boyfriends told them so. They feel that it's their responsibility to try harder to understand and show love even more. They try to change it by themselves. It takes a long time to realise that it's their boyfriend who must change his behaviour and she can't do it for him.

'I thought that if I loved him enough, he would change.'

'I love him more than anything in the world so I try harder to be what he wants.'

'It took me a long time to figure out that his temper had nothing to do with me. I couldn't change it no matter what I did or didn't do.'

Battering happens to many people whether others see it or not. So, you're not alone. There are problems and stresses within every relationship. Battering in whatever form it takes, is not an okay way to work things out and it's not something you should accept. Nobody deserves to be abused.

'He slapped me around one time when he thought I was after his best friend. We were just talking; I had no interest in his friend.'

The best way to stop abuse is by not accepting it; telling your boyfriend or date that it's not all right with you and stop the relationship. Staying in the situation is not going to help anybody and he may not even realise that his behaviour is wrong. Too often women believe that it's their responsibility as nurturers to stay and help keep the relationship together. But as long as they stay, their boyfriends have no reason to change.

'They all thought I was stupid to go out with him. They didn't know how much we loved each other.'

Conclusion:

The best way to stop dating abuse is by not accepting it. Tell your boyfriend or date that it is **not** all right with you and leave if they don't change. Staying in the situation is not going to help anybody and he may not even accept that his behaviour was wrong because that's how his parents interacted.

Talk to somebody - a friend, counsellor or a women's group. There are lots of people who don't understand or who may not even want to know about your situation, but don't be discouraged if you try to explain your situation to others and they don't help you. Keep on trying, because there are people who care. Nobody deserves that kind of abuse. There's always a way out. Therefore, 'Just say NO' to that kind of relationship.

Adult rape victims:

Rape, whether it's of a male or a female, is a terrifying act to the victim, no matter at what age the outrage takes place. Most suffer from Post-Traumatic Stress Disorder (PTSD) at least in the beginning. Almost twenty per cent of raped women never completely get rid of their PTSD symptoms.

The survey found that many more women were subjected to unwanted sexual events than were reported to police and/or community crime surveys.

Victims who felt they were in great physical danger during the rape were more likely to get severe PTSD than those who felt they were in less danger. If threatened with a weapon or raped by a stranger, they were more likely to get severe PTSD. Date rape often carries more physical violence for women. This is because the woman has a greater sense of security. After all, she knows the man and she is more likely to resist and fight back. The result can be a severe beating.

Others feel they had set themselves up for rape by 'doing something dumb,' so suffered from feelings of guilt and shame. Those who were raped when they felt they had 'done everything right' suffered greater anxiety because they saw the world as an unsafe place.

Some victims don't tell anybody, because they're afraid others will blame them for the rape. These individuals have not compared the woman's assault to other crimes. For instance, nobody would believe them or that they had 'asked for it,' if they were the victims of a robbery or if they were physically assaulted. Nobody wants to hear about a rape. The message seems to be, *'I don't want you to talk about it.'*

According to Queensland University of Technology research, women are reluctant to discuss unwanted sexual events because often they:

- Felt guilty or embarrassed;
- Considered it a private matter;
- Feared reprisals;
- Did not think they would be taken seriously; or
- Feared the court process.

How victims can be assisted:

Experts in this area advise that helping the victim re-experience the rape by talking about it, imagining it, re-creating it in their mind, is the best treatment. Most reveal that they have recurring nightmares, flashbacks and endless thoughts of how they could have handled the event better.

How can you assist a rape victim deal with their trauma?

- The rubber band on the wrist is a helpful technique. When they find themselves dwelling on the event, they snap the band, which gives their subconscious mind a jolt to keep it from going back to the negative thoughts.
- Give them instruction on how they can manage future anxiety. For example, they may have to deal with sudden

anxiety, if they see someone who resembles the criminal who committed the crime.

- Offer counselling that can help the victim handle everyday events.
- Encourage them to take self-defence courses.

After a few weeks, most can resume near-normal lives. They're better prepared to deal with issues that were frightening to them, such as going to places that they perceive are threatening or sleeping alone in their home.

Dealing with stalkers:

*(From the book: **I Know You Really Love Me** (Dell, 1998) written by Doreen Orion, MD).*

Stalking victims don't like to be called victims. They will say, *'I won't let myself be victimised,'* or, *'I'm not going to change my life because I'm being stalked.'* Sorry. Your life has changed. Forever. Unless you accept that, you will actually be helping the stalker.

You are a crime victim. The crime happens to be stalking. You must understand that the phrase 'stalking victim' says volumes about the perpetrator, but nothing about you. It does not tell us whether you stay at home in terror with sheets over the windows or whether you've decided to move away or to become active to change the laws in your state. On the other hand, accepting that you are a stalking victim serves to remind you that you must, from now on, take extra precautions that others do not have to take.

Here are some basics to start with:

1. Tell the stalker *'No'* once and only once and then never give him the satisfaction of a reaction again. The more you respond, the more you teach him that his actions will elicit a response. This only serves to reinforce the stalking.

2. Get a dog. The Los Angeles Police Department's Threat Management Unit says this is *'one of the least expensive but most effective alarm systems.'*

3. Block your address at DMV and Voter Registration. If you don't, anyone can get it for the asking.

4. Never give out your home address or telephone number. Get a post office box and use it on all correspondence. For those places that will not accept a post office box, change 'PO Box' to Apt.' and leave the number. Put this address on your cheques.

5. When the stalker gets your home telephone number, don't change it. Instead, always let an answering machine pick up. Get a new, unlisted number and give it to everyone who calls except the stalker. Gradually, only your stalker will be using your old number - it will become his private line. If it upsets you when he calls, put the machine in a room you don't use. You can even have someone else monitor the tapes. This way, the stalker will think he is still getting through to you, although you will never make the mistake of picking up when he calls. Whenever you close off one avenue for a stalker, he will find another and it could easily be worse.

6. Document everything. Even if you have decided not to go the legal route, you may change your mind. Keep answering machine tapes, letters, gifts, etc. Keep a log of drive-bys or any suspicious occurrences.

7. Take a self-defence class. A lot of security experts don't advise this, fearing that it gives victims a false sense of security - but we do. The best self-defence classes teach you how to become more aware of your surroundings and avoid confrontations; things that stalking victims would do well to learn.

8. Have co-workers screen all calls and visitors.

9. Don't accept packages unless they were personally ordered.

10. Remove any name or identification from reserved parking at work.

11. Destroy discarded mail.

12. Equip your gas tank with a locking gas cap that can be unlocked only from inside the car.

13. Get a cell phone and keep it with you at all times, even inside your home, in case the stalker cuts your phone lines.

14. If you think you're being followed while in your car, make four left- or right-hand turns in succession. If the car continues to follow you, drive to the nearest police station - never home or to a friend's house.

15. Never be afraid to sound your car horn or emergency button on your car door opener to attract attention.

16. Acquaint yourself with all-night stores and other public, highly populated places in your area.

17. Consider moving if your case warrants it. No, it's not fair - but nothing is fair about stalking. If you stay and fight through the legal system, you might get some justice (although not necessarily your definition of it) but you almost certainly won't get safety. There is no possibility of life imprisonment for stalkers. Research how to keep your destination secret. Stalking and victims' organisations can help.

18. Don't be embarrassed and think you caused this somehow. Stalkers need no encouragement. Your shame is your

stalker's best weapon. It makes you more likely to engage him or agree to plea bargains, which are bound to be taken as sympathy and we know where that leads. Instead, tell everyone you know that you're being stalked, from neighbours to co-workers, so that when the stalker approaches them for information about you, they will be alerted not to divulge anything and will let you know he's been around.

19. One young widow moved to escape her stalker, a stranger she had never really met. Yet, after finding out where she moved, he was also able to pinpoint her exact location by showing her helpful neighbours; pictures he had surreptitiously taken of her and her children, telling them that he was her estranged husband and she had kidnapped the kids.

20. Join one of the stalking victims' support groups that are springing up all over the country. They can be invaluable resources for information in your community (such as how local law enforcement handles these cases) as well as provide essential support. If there is no group in your area, start one. It only takes two people. Tragically, we can guarantee you are not the only person being stalked in your area.

Chapter 4
PORNOGRAPHY

The extent to which so many young people (boys most troublingly) can and do access the most confronting brands of pornography may occur at a time when their dealings with the opposite sex are very much a work in progress. Kids who are hooked on pornography can now receive a criminal record for sharing pornographic images.

Some males who have viewed pornography for years, find that they become impotent when trying to have normal sexual relations with a woman.

When they're apprehended, some child pornography users express relief because they did not believe they would be able to stop offending by themselves. Others express no remorse at all – have no feelings of guilt for their actions.

The downloading of child pornography is out of control with videos and still images becoming more extreme and showing increasingly younger children. The proliferation of smart phones and tablets has made it more difficult for parents to keep tabs on who their children are communicating with. Gone are the days when police could effectively advise parents to keep the home computer in a communal area, because the children have them with them at school and at friends' homes.

In July, 2015, Children's Commissioner Megan Mitchell has called for a review into whether Australian kids are being adequately protected from exposure to hardcore and violent pornography on-line. *'Children's ready access and exposure to violent and pornographic imagery through on-line platforms poses real risks of distorting their attitudes to sex and relationships,'* she said.

'I strongly support a review of how well regulatory and other measures are working to reduce the negative impact of pornography.'

She added that children needed better education, at home and school, about sex and healthy relationships, but other options such as opt-in porn filters need to be part of the solution.

Some governments are trying to block explicit pornography at a network level.

The dangers of pornography:

Watching pornography at a very young age can result in a completely warped idea of what normal bodies look like and how normal bodies react when another person 'turns them on.' Those who are addicted to pornography are completely unaware of what intimacy means and only see others as sexual objects. The idea of romance is foreign to them.

Many male teens compare themselves to how the 'stud's' anatomy is so much sexier than their own. They look down at themselves and realise that they fall short in the penis department. They look at their normal chests and biceps and compare them against the studs 'performing' in the pornography and again believe they fall short.

Distorted view of normal intimacy:

Females, young and old, shown in pornography look nothing like the average woman or girl, so the boys find they can't become sexually stimulated by normal-looking females, so revert back to masturbating while watching pornography or pay prostitutes for their services.

These males can't relate to females without wondering what she would look and act like if she was naked in bed. They have vivid pictures of this in their minds – and the girls often intuit this desire so become embarrassed and feel as if they've been mentally undressed.

Young boys who, through curiosity, put the word 'porn' into a Google search usually expect to see a couple having sex or simply show beautiful naked female bodies. Instead, they see savage sex performed on females; brutal acts that leave the woman battered and bruised. They see anal sex on young girls and boys.

The average Australian boy is eleven when he has his first exposure to pornography. Many innocently click onto what is known as 'gonzo porn' that shows anal sex, lesbians having sex and even gangbangs. Some are repelled by the visions, but others get 'hooked.'

Degradation of women:

The degradation of women, with violence and humiliation are shown in most of these sites. Many experts believe that porn has become a health emergency, not only for the teens and pre-teens exposed to it, but by the men who have grown up watching it and find that normal sex does nothing for them.

This kind of hard porn is no longer hidden, has become mainstream and it's now difficult for people to even find soft core porn on the internet.

Young teenage girls have their virginity taken from them by boys who have watched porn and think they have to mimic what they've observed on the porn sites. These young girls are often left with serious sexual injuries with vaginal and anal tearing.

The boys think this is how a relationship with a girl works and is mortified when her mother and father come to his home to explain to his parents the sexual and mental damage he has done to their daughter. The boy's shocked parents are often unaware that their son has been indulging in pornography (sometimes for years without their knowledge) let alone that he used violent sex on his fragile young virgin girlfriend.

As they mature these teens need higher and higher levels of violence to appease their appetite for watching sex that's all about punishment, domination and vengeance and there's nothing loving in the acts they're driven to perform. As grown men, they find it impossible to get or sustain an erection when they have to indulge in non-violent sex.

Parental role:

Parents play an important role in preventing kids from accessing hard-core porn. They need to have a discussion with their sons when they reach ten or so to explain the differences between normal sex and the kind of sex that is shown on pornography sites. Instead of pornography being the only sexual education received by vulnerable pre-pubescent children, we must start to fill the void so pornography does not become the sex education of our youth.

Parents are encouraged to install filters and software to block explicit adult sites. Unfortunately, as earlier mentioned, this does not protect their child from entering chat rooms – where there are no filters to protect them from pornography and/or predators.

Internet helps offenders:

While there is no doubt that the internet has made offending easier for those who would have offended anyway, it's also clear that it has increased the likelihood of people graduating from viewing child pornography to abusing children. Research is showing that pornography is by far the biggest indicator of what a person's actual preference is and if they have lots of porn, it's not going to help them stop re-offending. Someone who's viewing a lot of child porn is definitely going to be more at risk of committing offences against children. The more they see of anything, the more acceptable it's going to become – no matter what it is.

Some offenders start off viewing 'legal' porn, go to more bizarre things, moved on to bestiality, then children, and then move on to contacting children and finally they offend. If he started with pornography at around twelve or thirteen, by the time he's twenty-one or twenty-two he's trying to get kids through the internet.

In older paedophiles, the behaviour is ingrained; they've convinced themselves that they're not actually doing anything wrong. Then they meet with other like-minded men (usually on the internet) who share pornography which reinforces their idea that they're not doing anything wrong.

Gang rape is one of the many unwanted offshoots of men's growing pornography consumption. Growing numbers of gang rape victims is attributed to young men's consumption of pornography that fuels unhealthy views of sex. One young man will engage with a young woman for sex and then others are invited in – usually without the permission of the woman.

Chapter 5
DOMESTIC VIOLENCE

Everyone's human, and most people 'fly off the handle' at one time or another with their spouses. A husband may wonder if he might batter his wife if he was mad enough. Because of their nearness to each other, couples may find that their disagreements turn out to be shouting matches where neither member seems to hear the other person's side of the dispute. This often results in louder and louder responses until one member storms off in a huff, while another may resort to pouting and withdrawal. This can result in a vicious circle of conflict.

How safe is your relationship?

The following is a list of warning signals. If you (or someone you know) is with someone new and you notice s/he has some of these behaviours, it's a possibility that control and abuse may occur. Whether these have happened once or many times, these behaviours indicate their partner is choosing to use a system of power and control. Answering these questions may alert you to the level of danger in your (their) situation.

- Has your partner verbally abused you now or in the past?
- Has your partner physically assaulted you now or in the past?
- Does your partner have a history of violence?
- Does your partner always see himself as superior or always right?
- Does he use force or coercion to make you do things against your will?
- Does talking to members of the opposite sex result in unfounded jealousy and suspicion that is out of proportion?

- Does your partner need to know where you are constantly?
- Does your partner pressure you to have sex which is unpleasant, pressured or forced?
- Does your partner verbally degrade your self-worth by constantly putting you down?
- Does your partner fail to take responsibility for his actions and/or does he always blame you?
- Does your partner insist that you're always at home or only let you out of the house if they are with you or know where you're going?

Has your partner ever:

- Accused you of having affairs or being sexual with others?
- Acted like you are a possession owned by him?
- Smashed your belongings or broken things around the house, especially those of value to you?
- Punched holes in the walls or doors?
- Blamed you for his anger and violence, saying it was your fault?
- Monitored or limited your phone calls, conversations and e-mails?
- Checked the mileage on the car to see if he can work out where you've been or who you've seen?
- Threatened to leave you or told you to leave?
- Kept you from seeing family and friends?
- Taken away your money or controlled how you spend it?
- Refused to pay household bills or give you money towards paying for them?

- Called you fat or ugly or made you feel bad about the way you look?
- Said you were 'asking for it' after physically hitting or abusing you?
- Taken away the car keys from you?
- Used the children to threaten you. For example, told you that you would lose custody or never see the children again?
- Has threatened to: hurt the children, pets, a friend or members of your family or has already done so?
- Made you do something very humiliating or degrading?
- Insisted you dress more or less sexually than you want?
- Called you a whore, slut or other derogatory names?
- Made you have sex after emotional or physical abuse or when you were sick or in late pregnancy?
- Tried to control and confuse you with lies?
- Denied all responsibility for his behaviour?
- Pushed, shoved or pulled you?
- Slapped, kicked or punched you?
- Thrown objects at you?
- Spat, urinated of ejaculated on you?

If you have ticked **any** of these boxes, you are being abused - domestic violence is happening in your relationship. You are entitled to be safe. The more often you answered 'yes' - the greater risk you're in.

Wife abuse frequently happens after hours. Seventy per cent of reported assaults occur between 5:00 pm and 7:00 am. About half the incidents occur on weekends

Sixty-two per cent of all women murdered are victims of domestic violence.

Wife abuse is rarely a one-time occurrence. Each incident reduces the abuser's internal control and makes it more likely that another incident will occur. The more it happens, the more likely it is to happen again.

Beatings are frequently severe. About one-third of cases, medical treatment is required. Injuries include bruises, lacerations, fractures, burns, dislocations and scalds. Women have been attacked with fists, boots, broken bottles, knives, razors and belt buckles.

Cycle of abuse:

Domestic violence involves a cycle of abuse:

1. Husband/partner beats;
2. Husband/partner apologises - courts wife, gives gifts;
3. Honeymoon stage - wife may feel guilty that she made him feel so bad that he had to hit her. She feels the need to be punished for doing this; and
4. Repeat of the above.

As the cycle unfolds, the woman's endorphins are charged. This can affect her as if she was on drugs and when that cycle ends she has an emotional downer. The excitement associated with the danger has gone. This can be addictive.

She must replace those negative 'highs' with positive feelings related to the challenge of changing her environment and using her abilities to find a better way of life. Unfortunately, most women who came from battered homes don't know that life should be any different. Society needs to help them learn that there is a better way of life awaiting them. Television, newspapers and community services are slowly highlighting that domestic abuse is unacceptable.

One way of understanding abusive relationships is to see the violence as part of a larger cycle. Lenore Walker who has written '*The Battered Woman*' and '*Wife Assault Hurts All of Us*' offers a theory about this cycle of violence.

Rather than explaining what causes wife assault, the theory points to some reasons why women stay for years in abusive relationships.

Walker's cycle has three distinct phases: tension building, battering and remorse/contrite. One follows the next with no set length for any phase.

The tension-building phase:

Positive as well as negative experiences in daily living create stress. Stress and tension do not cause wife assault, but they can act as a trigger to abuse. Unresolved tension can cause anger and frustration to build and psychological abuse may become the outlet in the tension-building phase. Afraid of her partner's mounting anger, the abused woman may appear passive and accepting of the psychological abuse as a way of calming his anger.

Although the abused woman may appear passive and accepting on the surface, inside her, anger and frustration are building. Afraid that disclosing her feelings will cause further abuse, she becomes withdrawn. The more she withdraws, the more controlling her partner can become. As tension builds, the psychological abuse becomes more frequent and intense. In many abusive relationships, this abuse can occur daily until the tension becomes unbearable.

The abused woman may try to control outside influences to ease tension. Common examples of this are making excuses for his behaviour and avoiding contact with family and friends. This increases isolation and separates her from those who may want to help her.

The battering phase.

This is the phase where physical abuse takes over from psychological abuse. The battering phase may be triggered by the explosion of the abusive man's anger or by an external event. There is no way to determine how severe the assault will be because anger and frustration have reached the point where they seem uncontrollable. There is usually no way an abused women can stop the assault. The abusive man decides when the attack will start and stop. If she tries to fight back, she faces the risk of greater injury.

The battering phase is the shortest phase in the cycle of violence. It often lasts only a number of hours although some victims report battering incidents continue over a number of days.

Fear of further assault frequently stops the abused woman from seeking medical attention for her injuries. In many cases abusive partners knowing that their actions are criminal, wrong and may have consequences, prevent their victims from seeking medical help. If she does seek medical help, she may deny being abused.

Another reason why abused women do not reach out for help during the battering phase is that many suffer an emotional collapse within one or two days of the assault. Reactions, very similar to those of disaster victims occur. Feelings of shame, hopelessness and helplessness are common and abused women tend to remain isolated for a number of days after the assault.

Remorse/contrite phase (The honeymoon phase).

The tension that has built up is released in the battering phase. The honeymoon phase follows directly after the battering incident. Apologies for violence from the abuser, promises it will never happen again and his begging for forgiveness are all common in this phase. The abusive man may say he is sincerely sorry for the assault and both partners then may believe he will not be violent to her again.

Shelter staff usually see victims of wife assault as the battering phase is ending and the honeymoon phase is beginning. Women who have recently experienced severe physical and emotional traumas may be more motivated to consider making major changes in their lives at this stage.

Once the honeymoon phase is underway and if she has contact with the abuser, the victims' attitudes towards her situation often change. The abuser frequently reminds his partner how much he needs her. He reminds her that she will be breaking up the family if she goes or stays away. He attempts to convince her that even though he was wrong to beat her up, if he goes to jail, it will be her fault. He may threaten to harm her, the children, himself and others if she threatens to leave him.

Even though the abusive man may heap apologies, love and promises on his victim during this phase, she still suffers guilt and responsibility should he try to kill himself over what has happened (especially if he has tried suicide before) shame over not being able to keep her family together and; fear of spending her future alone. These factors work against the victim in the honeymoon phase and may make this the most difficult time for her to break the cycle of violence.

If the abused woman chooses to believe that the loving behaviour she witnesses during the honeymoon phase is the true indicator of what her partner is like, she will probably return to the relationship. Once she returns, the honeymoon phase may last for a number of days, weeks or months before the loving behaviour gives way to renewed psychological abuse and the cycle of violence continues.

Women who have remained with the abuser have reported that the period between assaults becomes shorter. In some cases the honeymoon phase disappears completely. With each new battering phase, violence becomes more severe and injuries more serious. Continued battering lowers her self-esteem and increases her isolation, making it more difficult to break the cycle of violence. It is important to note that minimising the abuse and especially denial of abuse and its effects, keep the cycle of violence going.

It's unfortunate that couples wait until one or both are considering separation or divorce to obtain marriage counselling. When couples face the threat that the quality of their marriage is in jeopardy - they need help. If they'd been aware of a workable communication technique early in their marriage, the situation might not have reached the stage where their marriage was in trouble or resulted in domestic violence or spousal abuse.

Domestic violence is the use of any form of violence by one person to control another and is used to describe any abuse that occurs in intimate relationships. Although domestic violence against men does happen, the cases are few and very far between. Unfortunately the same cannot be said about their female counterparts.

In the majority of cases of domestic violence, the victims are women. The abuse may continue long after the relationship has ended. Generally women in domestic violence situations do not enter into a relationship believing that it will become violent. There are occasions when women may make long-term relationship commitments believing that marriage or a marriage-like commitment will put a stop to extreme jealousy and possessiveness. There are also occasions when women enter longer-term commitments out of fear.

For many women, physical and sexual violence does not begin until a year or so into a long-term relationship, often during pregnancy. The controlling and dominating behaviour prior to long-term commitment is often interpreted as jealousy and often considered a compliment to the woman or a sign of his love for her.

Within a relationship, disagreements and arguments do occur - this is normal and both partners should be able to put forward their different points of view or concerns and discuss them together. It is not normal for one partner to feel threatened, too frightened to argue back or too frightened to disagree or express his/her opinion.

Many husbands cut off the support systems that may help assaulted women break the cycle of violence. Often the abuser convinces his partner that family contacts and friendships interfere with the relationship and make already existing problems worse. He may try to cut family ties, further isolating the assaulted woman. In extreme cases, women are forbidden to leave the home at all and if they are permitted to leave, it must be in the company of the abuser. Feelings of loneliness and despair for isolated women can further immobilise them from breaking the cycle of violence.

Almost half of all homicides are between spouses and most of the victims are women and come from a family where there was abuse.

Most men would argue that not all men are violent and that society shouldn't judge all men because of the actions of the men who are. Unfortunately, many of the men who condemn violence, abuse their wives and children because they don't consider their actions as being violent. Abuse that has its roots in childhood becomes part of a web of societal violence. Women are often fleeing mates who bring childhood abusive tactics into their adult relationships. They move from creating havoc in the classroom or schoolyard as children to being adults who create havoc in their homes. Regretfully, many child bullies mimic behaviours they have seen used by adults. These tactics seem to work - so they use them themselves.

The belief has been drummed into them, that men have the right to dominate women and thus, if they wish, they can abuse women. Fathers tell their sons, *'Don't hit your sister back - she's a girl.'* Millions of these small boys hear such comments from their fathers who then turn around and beat their mothers because supper is late.

Society's attitudes towards domestic violence:

Spousal abuse has remained an unrecognised crime for centuries. Wife abuse involves a husband intimidating his wife, either by threat or by actual use of physical violence. His violence may be directed at her person or her property. The purpose of the assault is to control her behaviour. Sometimes the fear of violence is enough to establish that control. Underlying all abuse is a power imbalance between the victim and the offender.

Some commonly held beliefs prevent a complete understanding of the problem of wife assault. Many people believe wife assault occurs infrequently and rarely results in severe injury. It is also generally thought that wife assault occurs only in low-income families, to poorly educated women or only in certain cultures.

We now recognise wife assault as a major social problem that affects thousands of women every year and experts agree that more wife assault occurs than is reported.

When we hear of assaults between strangers, we have little trouble recognising one party as the victim and the other as the offender. Our attitudes towards these assaults are clear. The offender is guilty of committing a crime. Society supports our attitudes by making offenders responsible for their actions and punishes them in order to protect their victims.

When we hear of assaults happening within relationships and families however, our attitudes are less clear.

Wife battering *is* a crime. Every citizen has the right to freedom from assault or from fear of assault. Wife assault involves the husband intimidating his wife, either by threat or by actual use of physical violence. The purpose of the assault is to control her behaviour. Sometimes the fear of violence is enough to establish control. Underlying all abuse is a power imbalance between the victim and the offender.

Abuse can be in the form of physical, sexual, psychological, destruction of property or pets and financial dependency. The longer the violence continues, the greater the chance is that the victim will experience all five forms of abuse. Survivors of wife assault, state their financial dependence on their partners was one of the main reasons for staying in the abusive relationships.

Financial abuse could be:

- Limiting access to cash and credit cards,
- Controlling PIN codes,
- Having sole access to bank and online accounts,
- Takint out joint loans without a partner's consent,
- Restrictint access to insurance, superannuation and estate planning documents,
- Making investment decisions without consultation,
- Asking a person to sign financial documents without explaining what they are

At one time in history, it was legal for a man to physically assault his wife as long as he did not use a stick any thicker than his thumb which is where the phrase 'rule of thumb' comes from. Although this practice has been outlawed for over a hundred years, societal attitudes are very slow to change and many of our beliefs about relationships between men and women remain outdated. Some of our attitudes not only allow, but expect husbands to dominate and control their wives.

In many relationships, wives may still be expected to obey and submit to their husband's demands. In relationships where physical violence is used as a method of control, our attitudes blur our ability to see wife assault as a crime. Instead wife assault is often viewed as a 'family problem,' to be dealt with by the family. When the victim recognises the assault as a crime, the guilt and humiliation she feels can sometimes stand in the way of her seeking help. As a result, thousands of women and their children continue to live in fear.

Fortunately attitudes are changing. The Women's Movement has been a driving force, increasing our awareness about wife assault. They have been a strong voice ensuring that women hear that equality in relationships is their right - not a privilege. Concerned individuals have worked hard to create shelters in our communities so that survivors of wife assault have safe places to go when they decide to reach out. Support groups for victims and offenders are established to provide a supportive network. Shelter services and other resources are available to people whether they choose to leave or remain in the abusive relationships.

The batterer, like a mugger, will deliberately choose a woman who seems least able to defend herself. Abused women don't go looking for thugs, but batterers can be very charming and can deceive them into believing that they're caring individuals. It's only after the woman has been exposed to his behaviour that a pattern begins to show.

Battering is not an occasional beating. It is a system of controlling a woman through terror, confusion, disabling and every imaginable brainwashing technique. Many battered women are prohibited from leaving their homes, forbidden to use birth control, prohibited from speaking with their friends and forbidden to work. They have no access to money.

Women who started out strong and self-reliant have been battered into feeling weak, powerless and totally dependent. Battered women are often deprived of sleep and become confused by their abuser's unpredictable actions and behaviour. This living in a constant state of terror is so debilitating that they lack the energy to think straight.

Women who are abused are found to have poor health, suffer chronic pain and depression, attempt suicide, have addictions and experience problem pregnancies in greater numbers than women who are not abused.

Often the abusing husband is cheating on his wife. She will know that this is happening when he picks on her, finds fault with her, tells others she is crazy or stupid, works out more, takes more pride in his appearance, hides money, becomes distant and addicted to the internet and/or phone.

Drug and alcohol abuse:

One of the most commonly held beliefs of the cause of domestic violence is alcohol or substance abuse. But the fact is that almost even numbers of sober and drunken men are violent. Where studies show that more drinkers are violent to their partners, the studies are not able to explain why many drunken men (80 per cent heavy and binge drinkers) did not abuse their wives.

In fact, men use alcohol or other addictive substances as a means to give themselves permission to be violent. If someone blames alcohol or drugs, they are avoiding taking responsibility for their actions. Many people enjoy drinking and some may even drink excessively and never get violent. Many people stop their drinking and still keep using violence and controlling behaviours. While the use of alcohol and drugs can often make the violence more serious - they do not cause it.

What about women who use violence?

There are a small number of women who use a pattern of abuse against their partners. There are also a small number of men who need protection from violence from either a female or male partner. Sometimes these men are ashamed or find it hard seeking help to be safe. However, most men report that they have been assaulted by other men, by a partner, adult son, father, brother or other.

Women's use of violence against their partners can take several forms:

- Self-defence - when women use violence to protect themselves.
- Retaliatory violence - when women hit back after experiencing a long history of abuse.
- Predominant aggressor violence - when women use violence as control.

Mutual violence:

Mutual abuse is not common. A 'fight' involving violence where both people are equal is rare. A pattern of violence that includes control and domination by one of the partners is more common. Where one person uses violence as a form of control, this person is known as the predominant aggressor.

Religion and domestic violence:

> 'The Scriptures can sometimes be misused to condone the use of power and to keep women and children in unsafe situations; hence care offered by the church has often been destructive rather than liberating.' (Ian George, Archbishop of Adelaide, 1995.)

When interpreting Bible or Koran texts, people may quote short passages out of context for their personal use. This can alter the meaning of the passage. Abusers may use their religion or religious affiliation as an excuse for their violence. ***Religion is no excuse for domestic violence.*** There is nothing to support the view that it is God's will for people to endure family violence. Some women may feel pressure from their faith or community to 'honour' their commitment to marriage and stay in an abusive relationship. They may think that to leave or get a divorce is against their religious beliefs.

Culture and domestic violence:

It's important to maintain cultural traditions and beliefs, but this can be done without violence or abuse. Some abusive men claim that in their culture, women have a subordinate role and the use of violence is permitted to keep women in line. Some excuse the legal system of attempting to destroy their culture or that laws against family violence are racist.

Young Muslim girls (some living in Australia) are still being mutilated by castration when they're only six or eight years of age. From a Muslim male's point of view, it is done so that women will remain pure, but they rob their women of the pleasures of lovemaking.

Respecting a person's culture is important, but stopping that kind of violence is more important. Under the law the same standards of non-violent behaviour should apply to everybody regardless of their cultural background or religion.

Conclusion:

Abuse in homes is a universal, albeit complex phenomenon, which has far-reaching effects. Women who are abused are found to have poor health, suffer chronic pain and depression, attempt suicide, have addictions and experience problem pregnancies in greater numbers than women who are not abused.

Domestic violence has its roots deep in the past and is anchored in many cultural mindsets, whether one is talking about traditional cultures or in the developing world. Although some change in attitudes is taking place, much more needs to be done and those who are abused need to learn how to 'Just say NO' to that abuse and find those who can help them leave their destructive environment.

Abusers believe:

- They should be in control of their partners and/or children.
- Their needs and goals are more important than those of other family members.
- The person(s) they're abusing are inferior or unimportant;
- There is nothing wrong with controlling and punishing certain family members.
- That certain family members should behave in particular ways.
- That the abused persons have negative intentions and motives behind their behaviours.
- They have a right to use abusive behaviour;

They:

- Have inadequate or inappropriate knowledge and skills.
- Are unable or unwilling to stop their abusive behaviour.
- Have had experiences in their lives that have caused severe psychological harm to them.

Their victims believe:

- They have no way to escape or stop the abuse.
- They deserve the abuse.
- That the abuser has the right to control and/or punish them.

Attitudes towards abuse:

The following information shows how things should be in an equal relationship. Neither partner needs to be the boss. Equality, trust and love must be paramount for there to be equality between men and women.

Economic Abuse:

- Keeps her from obtaining or keeping a job.
- Takes her money;
- Gives her an allowance or makes her ask for money;
- Gives her no knowledge of or access to family income.

Vs: Economic Partnership;

- Make money decisions together;
- Both partners benefit from financial arrangements.

Using coercion and threats; Makes and/or carries out;

- Threats to do something to hurt her or the children;
- Threatening to leave her and/or the children;
- Deny her access to her children;
- Threats to commit suicide;
- Will report her to welfare;
- Make her drop charges;
- Make her do illegal things.

Vs: Negotiation and fairness;

- Conflicts are solved by seeking mutually satisfying resolutions;
- Both acceptable to change;

- Both are willing to compromise.

Emotional Abuse;

- Puts her down;
- Makes her feel bad about herself;
- Calls her names;
- Badgers her until she thinks she's crazy;
- Plays mind games;
- Humiliates her, especially in public;
- Makes her feel guilty.

Vs: Mutual Respect;

- Listen to each other non-judgmentally;
- Are emotionally supportive and understanding;
- Value each others' opinions.

Intimidating;

- Makes her afraid by using looks, actions, gestures;
- Destroys things;
- Demolishes her possessions;
- Abuses pets;
- Shows weapons.

Vs: Non-Threatening Behaviour;

- Talk and act so she feels safe and comfortable;
- She can express herself and can do things without his permission.

Using male privilege;
- Treats her like a servant;
- Makes all the big decisions;
- Acts like 'the king of the castle;'
- He's the one who defines men's and women's roles.

Vs: Sharing responsibility;
- Mutually agree on a fair distribution of work;
- Make family decisions together.

Using children;
- To make her feel guilty;
- Uses the children to relay messages;
- Uses visits with children to harass her;
- Threatens to take the children away.

Vs: Responsible parenting;
- Shares parental responsibilities;
- Is a positive, non-violent role model for the children.

Minimising and denying abuse;
- Makes light of the abuse;
- Does not take her concerns about the abuse seriously;
- Denies that the abuse happened;
- Shifts responsibility for his abusive behaviour saying she caused it.

Vs: Honesty and Accountability;

- Accepts responsibility for abusive actions;
- Acknowledges past use of violence;
- Admits it when wrong;
- Communicates openly and truthfully.

Isolating;

- Controls what she does, who she sees or talks to; what she reads and where she goes;
- Limits her outside involvement;
- Uses jealousy to control actions.

Vs: Trust and support;

- Supports her life goals;
- Respects her right to her own feelings, friends, activities and opinions.

Why do men abuse?

Men get no instruction. The man has a corrupted mentality about his role. If a man believes that it is part of his duty as the head of the family to control what his wife does, then he may feel it is okay to hurt her. He may not know any other way.

Violence offers the man a quick solution to disagreementws. It helps him avoid talking about the real problem. And because men are physically stronger - they will win - so there won't be a problem the next time a similar problem arises.

We like to think of masculinity as natural, but most of its manifestations are cultural and historical - rather than biological. They get the myth of masculinity being how James Bond acts by defeating the other guys, seducing the women and burning down the buildings. Still, all that is masculine is not bad. We just need to tear away the trappings and define masculinity in different terms. Masculinity on the one hand has meant strength and activity in protection of the family, but on the other hand it has also meant escape from domesticity and resistance to the control of women.

The biggest advantage for women is that if they are having a problem coping, they seek help. Men don't. Emotionally, it's not part of their role. When the pressure becomes too much, they look for ways to relieve it through alcohol, drugs, overwork, hitting their wives/children or having affairs. When men are out of control with their masculinity, there are three kinds of behaviours they can portray that are harmful:

The Homoclyte.

This is the most insidious form of behaviour. Homoclytes are boring, rule-bound and afraid of their emotions. They have difficulty with intimate relationships. They live within a narrow range of emotions and they believe that set of emotions is right. That was the norm for men in the 1950s. More modern men may still feel that any man who shows his feelings is out of control.

Men's value has been stripped down. A common misconception is that all they are expected to do is make money, donate sperm and die, leaving their families well off. Their value is determined by how much money they make.

The root of the problem is that they haven't been fathered properly. Fathers today are usually too busy playing at being masculine to take part in raising their sons. What a boy might see is his father out there fighting wars, working or chasing other women, proving he's not under anyone's control. There's been no strong model for them about what it is to be a man. So when a boy reaches adolescence, he begins to define masculinity as anything that isn't female. He will tend to exaggerate these differences because there is no role model. And society's answer to masculine behaviour is often '*A man's got to be what a man's got to be.'* For some men, being masculine begins and ends with having a penis.

He feels Mom has the power to define whether or not he's a man and he begins to sense he has to escape her control. After all, she can remind him he's still a child. No matter how much he needs his mother, he doesn't want to be seen to need her. So he thinks that if he's dirty enough and loud enough he will feel masculine. He feels kinship only with other guys and if there are no grown men around, he will identify only with the other boys.

He turns to adolescent girls to have his masculinity affirmed. They don't know any more than he does. So much fear of female power comes from this time in a boy's life. It's a great set-up for infidelity, because in order to re-affirm his masculinity, he has to continue testing his sexuality by seducing other women. Men act out the script they were given. They don't know who created the script, but they follow it.

When women pushed for independence, the shoe was put on the other foot. Men had to deal with things they didn't have a script for. Part of the problem has been women telling them that they need to change. Yet men have been taught not to value females. Men have been blaming everything since Adam and Eve on women. What most of these men are trying to do is be masculine enough to get their father's approval. Most fathers' behaviour differs drastically from what has become the norm in society.

The Philanderer.

He has a desperate need to seduce women. And once he's done that - he discards them. The game is to score with women. A philanderer is basically very, very angry with women. He doesn't like them and that makes him dangerous. He's out to defeat them one by one. Unfortunately, women seem to be attracted to them.

The Competitor.

Life is a contest with the other guys. It all goes back to adolescence when he spent his time measuring his penis. This guy can make anything into a contest - how much money he makes, how many degrees his wife has, what his children have accomplished, his golf handicap and the kind of car he drives.

Conclusion:

It's not that men don't want to change. They just don't know how. If you ask a man to be more nurturing, he might really want to be. We're asking for a whole new masculine role. The question is - how can we make it happen? Perhaps the boys who have been raised in households with only a mother will be the ones helping make the shift to less gender identification of roles.

What to do if you're in an abusive relationship:

Making the decision to end the cycle of violence is a difficult one for the assaulted woman. Assaulted women cannot stop their partner's violence, however they can stop being victims. These women need to look beyond their own hellish life to the lives of their children because they are not the only ones that the violence cripples and destroys.

- They must get qualified medical help to learn how to deal with the horrific guilt feelings that cling to a person who has had to submit to such aberrant behaviour. They must believe that they were innocent victims of the abuse.

- They must learn how normal families function. They learn this by observing and talking with friends whose families display normal nurturing, loving behaviour. They would ask questions of close friends and seek their help in identifying any reactions to situations or behaviour others are portraying that appears different from how they perceive life.

- Then they need to put their past behind them. What happened in the past - is the past. They need to stop letting it influence everything they do and learn to stop themselves when they find themselves slipping into their former negative thinking.
- They need to set specific realistic goals for themselves and keep telling themselves that they *will* succeed.
- They need to write down and remember their successes. They would bring out their 'brag list' whenever they're having serious doubts about whether they can succeed or not.

Question: How do I know if he's changed?

Answer: Change comes slowly. Trust your gut feeling regardless of other signs. Ask yourself these questions:

- Has he completely stopped doing and saying things that frighten you?
- Will he listen to your opinions with respect?
- Can you express your opinions without fear of being punished?
- Does it feel safe to bring up topics that you know upset him?
- Does he respect your wishes about sex and physical contact?
- Has he stopped expecting you to do things for him?
- Can you spend time with friends and family without being afraid he will retaliate?
- Do you feel in control of your life?

If you're in a destructive relationship, learn how to 'Just say NO' to violence and take action to remove yourself from the danger.

Chapter 6
CHILD ABUSE

How can you identify child abuse?

The following indicators may help alert you to the possibility of abuse:

- Unexplained bruises, welts or injuries, especially in places that children do not normally injure during regular play or movement.
- Burns that leave a pattern outlining the object which was used to make the burn, such as a cigarette, an iron or an electric stove burner; burns on the hands, feet or buttocks caused by scalding water or rope burns caused by being tied.
- A child who is continually hungry, unsuitably dressed for the weather and/or always dirty.
- A young child who is often left alone.
- A child who is unusually aggressive, angry and hostile with other people.
- A child who demonstrates withdrawal behaviour, who refuses to participant or dress appropriately for physical activities.
- A child who shows unusual knowledge of sexual matters, who acts sexually provocative around adults or who shows unusual fear of a particular adult, adults of a particular sex or adults in general.
- A child who hints or talks about sexual abuse.

What is Child Abuse?

Abuse is defined in the dictionary as 'an evil or corrupt practice; deceit, betrayal, molestation or violation' and comes in many forms. All abuse is violent, be it physical, emotional, psychological or a combination. The common denominator of all abuse is the collection of behaviours related to bullying. There are seven types of abuse:

Sexual:

Is the improper exposure of a child to sexual contact, activity or behaviour. It includes any sexual touching, intercourse or exploitation by anyone in whose care the child has been left or who takes advantage of a child. Such a person could be a parent, a relative, a friend or a stranger. Sexual abuse of a child is a criminal offence. It includes incest, rape, buggery or any paedophile activity for the gratification of the abuser.

In cases of child abuse, the abuser usually has a sexually dysfunctional or unsatisfying relationship with his/her partner. Their sexual relations with their partner may be violent, inadequate or non-existent and the children may become convenient substitutes. Child abuse can begin when the mother is pregnant with another child and can't have sex.

Depending on its nature, its frequency and the child's relationship with the abuser, sexual abuse can have a variety of effects. The most serious are physical damage, feelings of betrayal, powerlessness, guilt, shame and confusion about sexuality and its expression. The increasing number of adults wanting counselling for childhood sexual abuse shows how long-lasting the effects of this type of child abuse are.

Physical:

Includes assault and any deliberate act resulting in physical injuries. This includes beating of children in the guise of corporal punishment - but which can be delivered with fists, through shaking or hits to the child's head. The intentional use of force on any part of a child's body that results in injuries is against the law. It may be a single incident or a series or pattern of incidents. The law states that physical force cannot be used on children unless the force used is 'reasonable' and has been used for 'corrective purposes' by a parent or someone acting in the role of parent.

Physical abuse can cause severe damage to children. That damage can be physical and/or psychological. It can take the form of permanent injury to a child's body as a result of broken bones, burns, shaking and being thrown about. Hearing can be damaged and mental functioning can be impaired.

Tactile:

Happens where there is little or no physical contact between parent(s) and the young child and any contact tends to be violent, punitive, unjust and inappropriate. Physical contact seems to be especially important in the first five or six years. Some children enjoy a cuddle into their teens. Sadly, with abuse coming into the open, many parents (especially fathers) now fear that physical contact with older children may be regarded and misconstrued as abuse.

Existence:

Where the existence and rights of the child are ignored through neglect of needs:

- Physical (food, clothing, shelter);
- Intellectual (education);
- Psychological (self-development, self-confidence, self-esteem, maturity);
- Behavioural (company, friendships, interpersonal and communication skills, relationships);
- Abandonment (leave child alone for long periods of time).
- Some ignore the child's existence or ignore one child and give love to others.

Religious or cult:

The child is forced to accept the narrow, exclusive religious views of the parent or guardian to the exclusion of any other belief or possibility of any belief. Any behaviour by the child not in line with the parents' rigid religious zeal is met with punishment and abuse. The child is subjected to strange, unnatural and often perverse beliefs on sexual matters and sexual development in line with the religious belief. S/he is discouraged or prevented from associating with any person not sharing the religious belief of the parent or guardian. In some cases, the child may be subject to genital mutilation and as an adult are forced to live in isolation behind veils.

Emotional neglect:

Is the failure to meet the child's emotional needs for affection and a sense of belonging.

Emotional Abuse:

Is anything that causes serious mental or emotional harm to a child. Emotional abuse may take the form of verbal attacks on a child's sense of self, through repeated humiliation or rejection. Exposure to violence or severe conflict in the home, forced isolation, restraint or causing the child to be afraid much of the time, may also cause emotional harm. Emotional abuse rarely happens only once. It is usually part of a particular way of relating to children.

Emotional abuse affects a child's developing sense of self. Humiliation, rejection and insults can result in feelings of worthlessness and lack of confidence. It can cause general feelings of anxiety and insecurity that can affect every area of the child's life. The effects may show up as aggression, delayed development, depression or withdrawal.

Children exposed to violence in their homes grow up with fear and insecurity. As well, they learn about the use of violence in close relationships and many grow up to repeat what they have learned.

Parents who deliberately withhold love - are unwilling or have an inability to express love. Others give conditional love - that unless their children conform, they won't be loved. They love one child to the exclusion of others. They smother the child and deny the opportunity for him/her to develop as a separate individual.

They force the child into conflict or use the children as a pawn between warring parents or witnessing violence between the parents. They place the child into a caretaker role at an inappropriate age. The child may be forced to witness alcohol or substance abuse or are forced to participate.

Psychological:

Parents give constant criticism or blame for trivial or unjustified reasons that may have no connection with the child. They refuse to acknowledge the child or their achievements and refuse to praise. Parents give unclear, shifting and inconsistent boundaries - sometimes no boundaries - and at other times give very tight boundaries.

They use the silent treatment with the child.

The child is exposed to the unpredictable behaviour of their parents. Psychologically, a child may feel unwanted, worthless and bad and may be violent with other people when s/he grows up.

Neglect:

Is any lack of care that causes serious harm to a child's development or endangers the child in any way. Neglect in its most extreme forms affects every part of a child's development. It can affect physical growth, mental development and emotional well-being.

Physical neglect:

Is the failure to meet the child's physical needs. This includes failing to provide adequate nutrition, clothing, shelter, health care and protection from harm.

Child abuse is anything that endangers the development, security or survival of a child. A child is anyone under the age of eighteen.

Another form of abuse: Smoking!

Smoke Gets in your Eyes - Excerpts from Elaine Hollingsworth's book **Take Control of your Health and Escape the Sickness Industry** www.doctorsaredangerous.com

The most vulnerable passive smokers are babies in the womb. With every puff, the amount of blood and oxygen going to the foetus is decreased. This is what creates brain damage. Five minutes after the mother has a cigarette, her baby's heart speeds up and breathing movements decrease. These are signs of foetal distress. Blood pressure is raised during and after smoking. This is harmful to both mother and child. The mother's risk of having a stillborn baby is significantly increased and she is 80 percent more likely to have a spontaneous abortion than a non-smoker. If she smokes, her baby's body and brain will weigh less at birth and its chances of mental retardation and birth defects, such as port wine stain, cleft palate and harelip, will be higher.

There is strong evidence of development problems later in life and the child's height may be affected. Lower IQ scores, reading disability, behavioural problems and hyperactivity are all seen in the children of smoking mothers. Nothing can excuse a woman who allows such life-threatening things to happen to her unborn child!

Babies have small lungs and very small airways, so smoke-filled air impairs their breathing. Babies and young children breathe much faster than adults, meaning they inhale more air

- and more pollution - in comparison to their body weight. Infants whose parents smoke at home have a higher rate of pneumonia and bronchitis. Many researchers have found that the dreaded sudden infant death syndrome can be passive smoking-related. Zinc, which is vital for healthy growth in babies, becomes deficient in babies who are forced to breathe tobacco smoke. The breast milk of smoking women contains significant amounts of nicotine.

Second-hand smoke diminishes the blood supply to the bones and cuts off vital nutrients and contains up to 150 times higher levels of carcinogens than smoke directly inhaled by cigarette smokers. All smoking pollution remains long after the smoker has stopped. Even when a smoker inhales, researchers have calculated that two-thirds of the smoke from the burning cigarette goes into the environment. Insidiously, side-stream smoke contains far more of the carcinogenic tars and smoke particles and concentrations of noxious compounds than the mainstream smoke inhaled by the smoker. This exposure is deadly, because the toxic and carcinogenic chemicals released from the burning tip of the cigarette enter the atmosphere totally unfiltered by a mat of tobacco.

Some studies show there is twice as much tar and nicotine in side-stream smoke compared to main-stream; three times more of a compound called 3-4 benzopyrene, which is a carcinogen; five times more carbon monoxide, which robs the blood of oxygen; and 50 times more ammonia.

There is also evidence that there is even more cadmium in side-stream smoke than in mainstream. Cadmium damages the air sacs of the lungs and causes emphysema. Once cadmium gets into your lungs, you've got it. It never goes away. 75 percent of the radiation in tobacco smoke enters the atmosphere and is inhaled by others. It is nothing short of criminal that smokers expose others [and especially their children] to additional, preventable doses of this deadly poison.

Doctors at the Royal Brisbane and Women's Hospital Research Foundation's Clinical Research Centre have found that smoking while pregnant blocks an adequate flow of iodine causing brain impairment in babies. Iodine is required to make thyroid hormone. Without iodine, the baby's brain doesn't develop as it should and results in lowered IQ levels. If babies don't have thyroid hormone, they can have very significant brain damage. Mothers who smoke ten to twenty cigarettes a day have enough thiocyanate in their blood to block the flow of iodine to their baby.

A shocking estimate is that twenty to thirty per cent of Australian women smoke during their pregnancies, affecting 76,500 babies born in Australia every year. To me, this is child abuse and the parents should be formally charged with the offence accordingly.

[Author's note. Why anyone, (male or female) knowing the dangers of smoking would start to do so - is beyond me. They need to learn how to 'Just say NO' to smoking!]

Societal passivity to sexual abuse at home:

In cases where a stranger commits child rape or abuse, society deals with it immediately and ruthlessly. But if a father, brother or mother commits the child rape or abuse, s/he rarely faces a jail term. If they receive a sentence, it's trivial when compared to stranger-child rape or abuse. This ***must*** change!

Physical and emotional child abuse is assault - and assault is a crime. Although most people in society would agree with this, somehow it remains deaf and dumb when it's faced with cases of incest. That assault not only destroys a childhood and removes sexual innocence, but sets the child up for a dysfunctional sexual future.

These children have bruises on the inside and there are few laws in place to protect them.

Reporting Abuse:

In younger children, maltreatment usually takes the form of physical abuse, in older children - neglect is more common. For child abuse to be reportable, parental behaviour must be inappropriate, dangerous and damaging. There is no law determining the age at which children can be left on their own, but authorities can remove youngsters if their safety is at risk. Parents who leave children in dangerous situations can be charged and the age of the child is immaterial. Parents need to consider not only the age but the state of their child's development.

We live in a society where other people care for children. The most common injury that's seen is bruises. Other signs of abuse include injuries in regular patterns, lacerations in unusual places, genital tears, burns, fractures of all kinds and head injuries. In most cases of abuse, the abuser inflicts the injuries using something within easy reach such as a belt or electrical cord. Hot water burns caused by placing a child in scalding hot water are among the common injuries.

Sexual abuse has ramifications for life. Children who are sexually abused have the whole fabric of their life changed. If daddy has sex with them every Wednesday night while mommy goes to bingo, for four years of their lives, it changes who they are and what they become. The definition of child sexual abuse is a child used as an object for the sexual gratification of the adult.

Then there's Munchausen where the parent receives reflected attention by making the child sick. Munchausen syndrome is a mental disorder in which the patient fakes illness to gain attention and sympathy.

Munchausen syndrome by proxy (MBP) is the old term for a form of abuse where the person either fakes or produces symptoms in someone else, usually their child.

Government Social Services departments have the legal responsibility to investigate all reported cases of suspected child abuse and take appropriate action. Some practices, which we once considered acceptable, are now believed to be abusive. If physical or sexual assaults are suspected, reports should be made to the police.

The role of society:

In our society, we expect parents and guardians to care for their children in a loving and nurturing manner. Unfortunately there are some who are unable or unwilling to do this. Parents and teachers who cling to the myth that children are best left to resolve their own conflicts or if their children fight back just once, the bullying will stop or children who bully will just grow out of it - may inadvertently be adding to the problem.

Some reports suggest that one in four households is a site of violence. Since children are unable to care for themselves, others in the community must watch for incidents and situations that might be harmful to them. Children of all ages, from infancy to adolescence, from any kind of home and background, can be abused. Infants have been sexually abused and adolescents have been beaten and humiliated. Such children are described as 'emotionally scarred'. Many young people who run away from home are doing so to escape abusive situations.

It's difficult for these children to concentrate at school. When children have to sleep in the car because they have been locked out of the house by an abusive parent, it's impossible for them to finish their assignments or study for the next day's test. It's difficult for them to develop trusting relationships with their teachers and peers. If we want to do more than pay lip service to the needs of children, we must spend less time scape-goating mothers and allocate more resources to investigating and improving the lives of children who live with violence, abuse and fear.

Children learn violence from adults. Children learn to be victims from adults. Ask any shelter worker about three- and four-year old boys who abuse their mothers, demanding juice, calling them 'Bitch,' and kicking them in the shins if they don't react immediately. And the tiny girls who cringe when strangers speak to them. These children grow up to be abusers and victims and they repeat the cycle with their own children. Some become abusive parents themselves. A few become paedophiles and rapists, unable to distinguish between normal, loving sexual behaviour and the predatory behaviour they experienced as children. A tiny minority become murderous psychopaths. Most serial killers have a childhood history of violent physical and sexual abuse. The emotional scars from such experiences may run far deeper than we would like to believe.

Domestic violence and children:

In homes where domestic violence occurs, children are also at high risk of suffering physical, sexual and emotional abuse. Whether they are physically abused or not, children who witness domestic violence suffer significant emotional and psychological trauma similar to that experienced by victims of child abuse.

Research confirms that abusive men often escalate violence to re-capture their partner and children who have sought safety in separation. The risk to children in the context of domestic violence separation is substantial. Yet the risk is virtually invisible.

While the impact of domestic violence on women has 'come out of the closet' over the course of the last twenty years, the impact and risk of domestic violence for children remains a closely held secret.

Women's shelters recognise that a child living in an environment where domestic violence occurs is an abused child. Not all children are affected by domestic violence in the same way. It can impact on every aspect of a child's life and behaviour.

Reactions of children exposed to domestic violence:

- Isolation:
- Feeling responsible for the abuse;
- Helplessness;
- Guilt for not stopping the abuse;
- Medical problems;
- Grief;
- Ambivalence;
- Fear of abandonment;
- Embarrassment;
- Pessimism about the future;
- Eating and sleeping disorders;
- Depression;
- Detachment;
- Fantasies about normal life.

Reactions of adolescents to domestic violence

- Poor grades, school drop-out;
- Low self-esteem;
- Refusal to bring friends home - stays away;
- Runs away;
- Isolated;
- Violent outbursts;

- Irresponsible decision-making;
- Eating disorders;
- Suicide attempts;
- Substance abuse and other delinquent behaviours;
- Unable to communicate feelings;
- Nightmares;
- Depression;
- Dating violence;
- Physical symptoms;
- A temptation to fight back no matter what the consequences.

When children are brought up under those constant conditions the areas of the brain, which control their interpersonal, behavioural and social skills fail to develop normally. The violence and sexual abuse in infancy and childhood can cause permanent changes to the structure and wiring of the brain that psychotherapy and drugs may not be able to repair.

Childhood abuse within the critical time when the brain is being physically sculpted by experience imposes severe stress that can disrupt its structure and function. Later in life these changes can cause depression, anxiety, suicidal thoughts and post-traumatic stress disorder. The children express their mental state through aggression, impulsiveness, delinquency, hyperactivity or drug abuse.

Borderline Personality Disorder (BPD) is strongly associated with ill treatment in early childhood. People with BPD tend to see others in black-and-white terms - almost worshipping them at one moment, then vilifying them for some perceived slight. They have almost volcanic outbursts of anger.

These damaged children lack the ability to control frustration or anger or to monitor or control violent behaviour. They take no responsibility or understood the consequences of their actions and show little or no concern for others. In many cases of violent offenders, their brain's ventral region of the frontal lobes - which modify and control violent rages, are measurably smaller than in normal people.

The key to successful treatment is to act as quickly as possible while the developing brain was most capable of adapting to change. Magnetic resonance imaging (MRI) is a powerful tool for examining brains. Several MRI studies have shown that, in abuse victims, the hippocampus is reduced in volume by an average of 12 per cent and seemed to involve only the left side. If some key function is damaged in childhood, it's well established that other parts of a child's brain can be developed to pick up such functions. Rigorous training in interpersonal and social skills and establishing rules of conduct would encourage other parts of the brain to acquire that control. In the future, genetic intervention to curb anti-social behaviour may be a possibility.

Children who have known no other way of life, may think their abusive environment is normal. They may blame themselves, believing that they have done something to deserve the abuse. Some abused children grow up to repeat the abusive child-rearing style of their parents. Others are fearful that they will be abusive parents and may refuse to have children for that reason.

Children are wholly dependent on their parent(s) and the parent(s) possess (in the eyes of their children) a God-like status. In the eyes of the child, his/her parents can do no wrong and become his/her role models. Therefore, when a child is smacked - s/he doesn't know it's not the way his/her behaviour should be corrected. S/he may feel that, *'I'm bad, so*

I'm therefore being justly punished.' No person can ever be bad; it's their behaviour that's bad. The lesson that it teaches is that violence is an acceptable solution to problems.

For many, relief from their pain - or their memory of pain from corporal punishment, can only be obtained by doing the same to others. This is known as displacement aggression. He hit me and I can't hit him back, so instead I'll hit somebody else. The child who is subjected to regular abuse needs an outlet for his/her aggression and may act out violent impulses on another child at school, a sibling or a family pet. Violence towards animals such as torturing a cat or killing a dog is now recognised as a common early warning sign of forthcoming violence in adulthood.

Behavioural problems:

Some children who live with violence become aggressive. Uncontrollable anger is a common outlet for feelings that are otherwise difficult to express. For some, there is a tendency to never be seen as weak or needing help from anyone. Angry children are very good at hiding their need for love and security.

Other children show opposite behaviour and become withdrawn and fearful. Direct attacks from their parent's anger are often handled by running or hiding, shocked silence and clinging. These children can be very passive and easily withdrawn. Children and teenagers from violent homes may become depressed and the risk of suicide cannot be ignored.

Children who learn to accept violence and aggression as normal in their families often avoid forming close relationships with others. The message they get from their parents is twofold. Firstly, relationships are seen as being based on manipulation and submission rather than love and mutual trust; secondly, those whom you love and trust hurt you the most.

Children often blame themselves for the abuse they witness in their families. Some experience guilt, feeling they should have endured the punishment rather than their mother. It is common for these children to seek punishment through other behaviours such as lying, stealing and throwing temper tantrums.

Children who witness or experience abuse may also have problems dealing with authority. Running away from home and failing in school are two examples of problems related to dealing with authority.

Counsellors and therapists who work with children who have behavioural problems now recognise that many of these problems are directly related to living in violent homes.

Conclusion:

We are becoming more and more aware of the damage, both short- and long-term, that is inflicted on children through domestic violence and abuse. Finding a solution to this problem requires action by both the families and society at large. It is only through such action that we can break the cycle of violence that sees children who were abused grow up to become abusive adults in turn. Children need to be taught that abuse is wrong and to report such abuse to a trusted adult.

If you observe or suspect that child abuse is taking place – do something! Contact Domestic Violence hotlines, your local police or Crime Stoppers, but don't let it continue. Just say NO' to child abuse by doing something constructive to stop it from continuing.

Chapter 7
ELDER ABUSE

The abuse of older people is an issue of growing concern for our community, as our population ages and the number of people vulnerable to abuse is increasing.

- Elder abuse is a form of family or domestic violence that is experienced by older people.
- Older persons, whose decision-making is impaired, are particularly vulnerable to abuse.
- Elder abuse is any abuse and neglect of persons age 60 and older by a caregiver or another person in a relationship involving an expectation of trust.

Elder Abuse is a relatively recent term for a form of mistreatment that, in reality, is just one part of a spectrum of violence that occurs when differences in power exist in relationships between people. Simply put, where there is an imbalance of power in a relationship there is a risk of abuse occurring from the dominant person or persons. These power differences have been interpreted, particularly in relation to domestic violence, as the result of living in a patriarchal or male-orientated society where males and male values dominate.

This type of gendered analysis of power and violence can easily be justified by noting that, in all age groups, the majority of those being abused are female while the abusers are mainly male. However, this gendered view of violence and abuse becomes blurred somewhat when the abuse occurs in older populations.

Even though there are more women than men in older populations, older women are still more likely to be abused than older men.

Barriers faced by elders:

In western societies there appears to be a general negative attitude towards ageing and older people; a manifestation of which is the often patronising stereotypes of older people portrayed by the media. These attitudes create a fertile ground for age discrimination and like any form of discrimination it devalues and disempowers the group it is directed against.

Other factors such as language barriers, access to culturally appropriate services, lack of a support infrastructure within some community groups, make detecting and responding appropriately to abuse in these communities a major challenge.

Rural and remote communities present another set of challenges associated with distance, availability and access to services and the understated issue of maintaining confidentiality within small community groups.

Responding to abuse in older populations therefore requires a very flexible and community-based approach to accommodate the different types of abuse in various cultural groupings and in remote communities.

Elder abuse is mistreatment of an older person that is committed by someone with whom the older person has a relationship of trust such as a partner, family member, friend or carer. Elder abuse may be physical, social, financial, psychological or sexual and can include mistreatment and neglect.

Elder abuse can happen to anyone. As with other types of interpersonal violence, elder victims are never responsible for their abuse, their perpetrators are responsible.

Vulnerability:

Some families and individuals, however, may be more at risk than others. Factors that may increase an elder's vulnerability include:

- Social isolation/loneliness (lack of social support networks).
- Mental impairment (may increase dependence on abuser).
- Personal problems of abuser (emotionally or financially dependent on the victim; history of mental illness;hostility; alcohol or drug abuse).

Identifying abusers:

Unfortunately, abusers are not always easy to spot. Adding to the problem, victims may not be physically or mentally able to report their abuse, or they may be isolated and too afraid or ashamed to tell someone.

The great majority of abusers are family members - most often an adult child or spouse.

Abuse can also occur at a long-term care facility, such as a nursing home or assisted living residence. Employees and temporary staff who have direct contact with residents are the most frequent perpetrators.

Other offenders may include other family and old friends, newly developed 'friends' who intentionally prey on older adults, and service providers in positions of trust.

What are the warning signs of elder abuse?

Here are some signs that there may be a problem:

- Abandonment: Desertion of a frail or vulnerable elder by anyone with a duty of care.
- Physical abuse: Use of force to threaten or physically injure a vulnerable elder such as punching, hitting, slapping, burning etc.

    (Slap marks, most pressure marks and burns or blisters - e.g., cigarette burns.)

    Explanations that don't seem to fit with the pattern of physical injury are also suspect.

- Withdrawal from normal activities, unexplained change in alertness, or other unusual behaviour may signal emotional abuse or neglect.

- Emotional abuse: Verbal attacks, threats, rejection, isolation, or belittling acts that could cause mental anguish, pain, or distress to an elder.

- Sexual abuse: Sexual contact that is forced, tricked, threatened, or coerced upon another person, including anyone who is unable to grant consent.

  (Bruises around the breasts or genital area and unexplained sexually transmitted diseases can occur from sexual abuse.)

- Exploitation: Theft, fraud, misuse or neglect of authority, used as a lever to gain control over an older person's money or property.

  (Sudden changes in finances and accounts, altered wills and trusts, unusual bank withdrawals, checks written as loans or gifts and loss of property may suggest elder exploitation.)

- Neglect: A caregiver's failure or refusal to provide for a vulnerable elder's safety, physical, or emotional needs.

- Untreated bedsores, need for medical or dental care, unclean clothing, poor hygiene, overgrown hair and nails, and unusual weight loss are signs of possible neglect.

- Self-neglect: An inability to understand the consequences of one's own actions or inaction, which leads to harm or endangerment.

If you have concerns about someone - trust your instincts. Don't be afraid to ask questions. Keep in mind that victims of elder abuse may be experiencing other problems and more than one type of abuse.

How can I tell if someone is being abusive?

While there is no typical profile of an abuser, the following are some behavioral signs that may indicate problems:

- Abusing alcohol or other drugs.
- Previous criminal history.
- Mental illness.
- Longstanding personality traits (bad temper, hypercritical, tendency to blame others for problems).

What actions identify elder abuse?

- Controlling elder's actions: whom they see and talk to, where they go.
- Isolating elder from family and friends, which can increase dependence.
- Emotional/financial dependency on elder, inability to be self-sufficient.
- Threatening to leave them alone or send elder to a nursing home.
- Appearing to be indifferent to elder, seeming apathetic or hostile.
- Minimising an elder's injuries, blaming victim or others for the abuse, neglect, or exploitation.
- Threatening to harm an elder's pet.
- Calling the elder names.

In long-term care settings:

Some other potential risk factors of elder abuse in long-term care are:

- Reliance on staff who lack compassion or empathy for older people and those with disabilities.
- Too few staff, high turnover and inadequate training.
- Negligent hiring practices (hiring violent criminals, thieves, and drug users to work as aides, maintenance workers, etc.; failing to do required background checks.)

Elder Self-Neglect:

Self-neglect in later life refers to the inability or failure of an older adult to adequately care for his or her own needs, behaviour which puts him or her at risk of serious harm or abuse by others.

A significant proportion of adult protective services cases investigated by authorities involve self-neglect - in some states more than half of all cases of elder abuse fit this category.

Signs of self-neglect can include:

- Lacking food or basic utilities.
- Refusing medications.
- Hoarding animals and/or trash.
- Unsafe living conditions, insect or vermin-infested living quarters.
- Poor grooming and appearance (soiled or ragged clothing, dirty nails and skin.)
- Inability to manage finances (frequently borrowing money, hiding money, giving away money and property, not paying bills.)
- Isolation, lack of social support.
- Disorientation, incoherence.
- Alcohol or drug dependence.

If you know or suspect someone is being abused, you can...

- Let them know that help is available.
- Invite them to talk in a place where they are alone and safe, and listen to them.
- Let them know it is not their fault.
- Respect their right to make their own decisions.
- Avoid being critical of the abusive person.
- Keep providing support, even if they refuse help.

How to obtain help in Australia:

- In an emergency, phone your emergency hotline in Australia - 000. *
- Call the Elder Abuse Helpline: for free and confidential advice for anyone experiencing elder abuse or who suspects someone they know may be experiencing elder abuse. Phone: 1300 651 192 (Queensland only) or (07) 3867 2525 (rest of Australia).
www.eapu.com.au/Welcome.aspx
- Legal support for seniors
https://www.qld.gov.au/seniors/legal-finance-concessions/legal-services
- Office of the Public Guardian: looks after the interests of adults with impaired capacity
www.publicguardian.qld.gov.au/adult-guardian
- Other support services for seniors:
https://www.qld.gov.au/seniors/safety-protection/support-services

* In Canada and the USA the emergency hotline is 911, in the UK 999.

Conclusion:

Help our abused elders by being observant and take action if you see it occurring. 'Just say NO' to elder abuse by reporting it and supporting the abused elder throughout the process.

Chapter 8
SOCIAL MEDIA

The dangers of social media:

Many teens and pre-teens use social networking websites such as Facebook, MySpace, Bebo, Twitter, Linkedin and ProfileHeaven to keep in touch with friends from school, camp, church or work. Teens also use them to strike up conversations with strangers - teenage and otherwise - whether they're seeking help with their homework, advice about a problem or a date for Saturday night.

Facebook was launched on February 4th, 2004. It was initially meant to be used only by Harvard students, but it soon went viral and is now world-wide. With 1.8 billion users in August, 2015, it has been a huge success. However, with so many people having access to this social media, *it is no longer safe for individuals to use it to communicate with friends.*

Facebook and other social media outlets are a godsend for companies and organisations wishing to let the world know about their product or service, but individuals should ***not*** be using it to communicate with others. For example:

My 15-year-old granddaughter lives in Canada (I live in Australia). She has listed me as one of her 'friends' on Facebook. I use Facebook to send my monthly newsletter to over 800 people. I have never met these people – they have subscribed to my newsletter via my website.

If my granddaughter sends me a message and I either click 'like' or send her a message – all 800 of my 'friends' will see her message. If they respond, all their 'friends' will also have access to my granddaughter leaving her open to being approached by thousands of people. All it takes is for one to be a paedophile!

> *Remember that if s/he posts something and a friend 'likes' or comments on it, his or hir post gets seen by all of that person's friends as well. Then someone else comments and all that person's friends see it too. As a result - within minutes of him or her posting it, their post may be seen by hundreds, even thousands of people she doesn't even know!*

Adults too are in danger, by being exposed to identity fraud and stalking by unsavoury people, so they too should not use social media as a method of communicating with their friends.

> *Children need to be very careful when they go on-line, especially going into chat rooms.*

> *Parents can stop their children from going into adult sites, but can't stop them from using chat rooms.*

> *One in four children using chat rooms on the Internet will be solicited by a child predator.*

Adult **cyber-harassment** or **cyber-stalking** is not cyber-bullying. Once adults cyber-bully children or try to lure children into offline meetings, it's called **cyber-harassment** or **cyber-stalking.** It is also called **sexual exploitation** or luring by a sexual predator. This is why it's extremely important that children and adults do not give out personal information on Facebook or any of the other internet media sites – better yet – don't go on them at all!

> *It's extremely important that children and adults do not give out personal information on Facebook or any of the other internet media sites.*

Chat rooms:

Chat rooms are full of paedophiles that prey upon children. For instance, a twelve-year-old girl told a girlfriend that she was corresponding with a fourteen-year-old boy on the internet. He had sent a picture of himself and wanted to meet her at a local McDonald's. She wondered if she should meet him. It was fortunate that the girlfriend's mother was a volunteer with Crime Stoppers who encouraged the girl to talk to her parents for advice as to whether she should meet him or not. Her parents called the police for advice and they arranged to have undercover police officers at the restaurant when she met the boy.

As they suspected, the boy was a grown man, a paedophile, who was arrested at the scene. The man had a prior record and had earlier been jailed for raping two young girls. So children need to know they should not give strangers any personal information over the internet and should be very cautious about meeting anyone they meet on-line. This man knew where she lived, what school she went to and how old she was.

The police obtained a warrant, searched the man's home, confiscated his computer and learned that he was stalking three other young girls and had already asked them to meet him. The police were able to contact the parents of those girls to warn them about the danger the girls were in.

The police computer experts also examined the information on the four girls' computers and were able to catch a paedophile gang who traded information about the young girls.

Paedophiles go on-line to seek tips for getting near children - at camps, through foster care, at community gatherings and at countless other events. They swap stories about day-to-day encounters with minors. And they make use of technology to help take their arguments to others, like sharing on-line printable booklets to be distributed to children that praise the benefits of having sex with adults.

What is a paedophile?

A paedophile is a person who has a sustained sexual orientation toward children, generally aged thirteen or younger. In most cases, the paedophile is at least sixteen years of age and at least five years older than the child. We know that paedophiles are overwhelmingly male, that their desire can fluctuate and that there can be some effectiveness in anti-libidinal medication to curb or reduce their sexual reactions, although researchers still hotly contest its efficiency.

Paedophilia is defined as a paraphilia which includes recurrent, intense sexually arousing fantasies, sexual urges or behaviours that involve children, non-human subjects, other non-consenting adults or the suffering or humiliation of oneself or one's partner.

Some paedophiles refrain from sexually approaching any child for their entire lives. At one end of the spectrum are those who prefer having sex with children – paedophiles – while at the other are people who will have sex with children because of the particular situation they find themselves in. It could be just out of curiosity; it could be because they don't feel as if children are going to judge them like adults will; it could be that they'll have sex with anything and children are just one of the spectrum; it could be a revenge-type scenario – he's in a relationship with somebody but feels disaffected in some way; doesn't have any power or control or feels as if his partner is dominating him – so he chooses children.

There are some who demonstrate a life-long fixation; it's their primary sexual focus. There are others who are periodically attracted to children, but not all the time. Some paedophiles will be repulsed and seek to avoid it, and others will give way to it because sexuality is a powerful driver of human behaviour.

Paedophilia can be characterised as either exclusive or non-exclusive. Exclusive paedophiles are attracted only to children. They show no interest in sexual partners who are not pre-pubescent children. Non-exclusive paedophiles are attracted to both adults and children. A large percentage of male paedophiles are homosexual or bisexual in orientation to children, meaning they are attracted to male and female adults and/or both male and female children.

They place themselves in positions where they can easily meet children. The internet has become a common hunting ground to prey on children. Today more and more kids are using Facebook accounts. By creating a profile displaying one's personal information these children are indirectly helping paedophiles find their next target. They can befriend children and manipulate, trap and lure their targets into a false sense of trust.

How they contact their targets:

Some paedophiles may **pretend they're someone else**, such as a classmate. Others develop friendship with children and then arrange times and places so they can act upon and fulfil their sexual desires.

Most people imagine paedophiles as ugly old men dressed in trench coats, hiding in the bushes, waiting to snatch young children off the street. However, recent television shows have exposed paedophiles as local neighbours, trusted friends, clergy, babysitters, teachers and even family members.

Female paedophiles:

Many people assume that only males are paedophiles, however female paedophiles do exist. These female predators display similar behaviour such as irrational thoughts, repetitive thoughts and many suffer from psychiatric disorders or substance abuse problems. Also, there's a higher likelihood that they've been sexually abused as a child. As children, they lacked the ability to control the situation. By sexually assaulting children, paedophiles attempt to re-live the trauma they experienced and learn how to master it. A complete role-reversal that in their minds gives them the upper hand and prevents them from being targeted again.

Church child abuse:

The Catholic Church frowns upon certain sexual behaviour with children. A great deal of hypocrisy surrounds the sex abuse scandal in the Catholic Church. In many cases, the clergy were paedophiles. These priests sexually abused minors, primarily male altar servers and exerted power over these boys. Yet Catholic children still remain vulnerable to sexual offenders regardless of their public façade.

The children who fell victim to the clergy were easily accessible, vulnerable and unthreatening. These priests who engaged in sexual behaviour with youth should be held responsible for their actions. The Church, police and the courts should take the proper steps to correct this type of behaviour and have their paedophilic priests seek treatment for their disorder and be kept away from children.

Grooming the target:

There are patterns to paedophiles' manipulations; consistent techniques by which they groom the trust of the child and those around them. Often the child knows the abuser and the man is able to offend through that position of trust. So, a parent or step-parent could be the abuser. It could be a mentor or sports coach or often through friendship or association with the family. ***The child is encouraged to keep secrets*** and the paedophile tries to isolate them from other people. Some may offer bribes.

Abusers find areas of common interest with the child; they flatter their intelligence and insight, give them gifts and pay attention to them more than their parents do. They conspire to create situations where they and the child will be together. Isolation is important to the paedophile – not only does it lessen the chance of detection, but forms a false but flattering sense of conspiracy with the target.

There's no type of child who is more vulnerable than another; targets come from all sections of society and different types of families – not just broken homes as is commonly thought.

Contact rate of paedophiles:

A report of data collected by school authorities in Canada identified that:

23% of middle-schoolers surveyed had been contacted by e-mail;

35% in chat rooms;

41% by text messages on their cell phones.

Fully 41% did not know the identity of the perpetrators.

Other contact methods of communication:

So how should children and adults keep in touch with their friends? They would use e-mails where they would send bulk e-mails to the friends they wish to contact. They, of course, could pass on the information, but not in the manner it would be passed on via social media.

Paedophiles don't always use the internet. Some may stalk children by following them. Many parents transport their children to and from every event, but some have to trust that their children will be safe going to and from school and/or events. These parents should try to arrange (possibly with school assistance) for groups of children who live close by to travel together, hopefully with other older students who can keep an eye out for anyone who looks suspicious. Or parents could share car-pooling to pick up and deliver children.

Internet safety:

Paedophiles seek a target-rich environment for finding their prey and the Internet has become their stalking ground. Think about it like this; would you ever let a stranger go up to your child's bedroom and talk to them alone for four hours? Would you ever leave your child alone in a park and come back four hours later?

To ensure that your children and household are safe from the threat of these predators, parents need to know how to protect their children:

- Have a serious talk with your pre-teens and teens about communicating through social media. Now that most children have a mobile phone, parents don't have the control they once had to keep their children off dangerous sites. Therefore, it's imperative that they discuss this chapter with them. The ideal situation would be that children would not have access through their phones to the internet.

- If that can be established, encourage them to use a home computer but don't leave your child alone in a room with a computer connected to the Internet. Any Internet-connected computer should be in the community part of the house. It should only be used when parents are home and can monitor their children's activity on the computer.

- It's a myth that a child on a computer at home is safe. At the least, they may be exposed to sexually explicit materials, and at the worst, they can be lured by an Internet paedophile.

- Parents should educate themselves on basic computer knowledge. They should be the ones who set up all Internet accounts and passwords. Make sure you know your child's account name and password. You should also be aware of any other e-mail accounts your child may have.

- Be aware. Parents should be cautious if a child suddenly closes a browser window on the computer when the parent enters the room, or if the child doesn't want the parent to see what s/he's working on. If the parent questions what the child is looking at, they should go to the computer and click the back button on the tool bar or lean over and look closely at the computer screen. Parents should also be aware of pictures coming in over the computer.

- Take the time to learn about Internet filters, firewalls, monitoring software and other tools. <u>Use your browser history, cache and cookies to find out what sites your</u>

children have been visiting. Enter their names, including nicknames, into popular search engines to see if they have public profiles on social networking sites. Do the same with your address and phone number. You might be surprised by how much of your personal information is on-line!

Locking certain computer sites doesn't work. Computer filters don't work for chat rooms, because there are no blocks for chat rooms. There is software to monitor a child's activity, but not their chat activity.

- Caution them to never, ever give out personal information over the Internet. This is a good practice for both children and parents. It makes it easy for people to find out about them if they have provided them with any personal information. If they need to give some information, only give their state identification. Never give out their city, birthday, name, or school they attend.

- Children should never upload a picture of themselves (selfies) onto the Internet via social media or e-mail. They should never e-mail a picture to a new 'friend.' Once the picture leaves their computer they have lost control of what can be done with the picture. A predator can do anything they want with it. So, stop your children from taking and distributing 'selfies.'

- Make sure you have open lines of communication with your children. Oftentimes children are communicating with strangers because there's no communication in the home. Have open discussions with your children so they feel comfortable talking with you. They should know that if they receive material that bothers them or if it's inappropriate, they should bring it to your attention so it can be reported to local law enforcement. They need to feel comfortable doing this.

- Many times, children feel they did something wrong or something they weren't supposed to do, so they think they'll lose computer privileges because of this. It's important for them to know that they can bring it to their parents' attention without getting into trouble.

If you suspect your child is in trouble:

Look for these signs:

- A child that starts to act differently, withdrawn, getting bad grades or spending a lot of time on the Internet. Many times, children will think they have found their new 'best friend' and they believe that this person will rescue them from their doldrums.
- If gifts start arriving at the home, this should also be a clue that something is not right. If your family starts receiving phone calls from people you don't recognise, this could mean there are serious problems. Either the child gave the predator your phone number or the predator found it. This can signify a threat to your child as well as the entire family, especially if the predator knows where you live.
- If you suspect your child could be the target of an Internet paedophile, call your local law enforcement agency immediately.

Stranger Danger

Teach your children about 'stranger danger.' As scary as it may be, parents need to talk to their children about people who might want to hurt them. The best way to protect your children is to get them involved in their own protection:

- Parents need to be aware of possible predators. Typical signs are: someone who seems too good to be true; who offers extensive help to your family; who knows too much about your children or children in general; especially if they don't have children of their own. You should know every adult who is allowed to have contact with your child.

- Talk to your children about paedophiles as soon as they can understand what you mean. As early as three to five years of age. When children begin to interact with the world, they're subject to being targets.

- Tell your child you love them no matter what. Remind them that they can tell you anything and you will still love them with all your heart.

- Don't be afraid that you're scaring your children, but don't ask them to deal with adult issues either. Speak to them in age-appropriate language and give them instructions about what to do. They will feel empowered by knowing how to protect themselves. Be careful sharing your own experiences if you were a target of sexual molestation for example. Providing too many details and rehashing the tragedy can create a sexually charged environment and be harmful for your children in the long run.

- Children need to know that they have the right to say 'No,' yell, or ask for help. It may contradict what they know about respecting adults, but tell them if they feel threatened, they have your permission to make a scene, or to run away to a public place. And they need to know they won't get into trouble if their fears were unwarranted. Let them know that no one has the right to hurt them or touch them inappropriately. Teach your child to call you if a stranger arrives when there are no other adults around.

- Make sure your children know what acceptable behaviour is and what is out-of-bounds; that there are private areas of their bodies that no one else should touch.

- Rehearse your child's response to danger. If s/he doesn't practice it, your child won't really know what to do. Telling your child to yell for help isn't enough. In the face of danger, a child could forget, so rehearse, role-play and practice what your child should do.

- Remind your children that predators don't necessarily look scary or strange. A dangerous person could look like the person next door, or even be someone they know.

Addressing the disadvantages of social networking:

The disadvantages of social networking and social media will continue to be studied for decades to come. In the meantime, we already know it's a significant source of concern among privacy advocates as well as parents who worry about their children's safety. But clearly, the disadvantages of social networking go much deeper than privacy and safety.

In his book '*Lightweb Darkweb; Three reasons to reform Social Media before it reforms us*,' Raffi Cavoukian provides an abundance of evidence to suggest needed reform. He challenges parents, educators and citizens to see the connection between youth development and what he describes as a 'vast sociological experiment' that may forever change human relationships.

The '*Lightweb*' is known to all who use the Internet as a daily part of life. We easily connect to anyone around the world, not just via e-mail, but through a variety of on-line platforms and texting applications even on the smallest personal computing devices; we have access to a global storehouse of information; powerful search engines find documents, arguments and historical precedents, and almost any on-line question finds answers; we connect by audio and video with anyone, for free; we can build an on-line music and entertainment library without leaving home; we have palm-sized devices with dazzling capabilities for learning, recording, sharing and connecting.

The '*Darkweb*' is there too. Imposters, predators and porn sites lurk in the shadows on the Information Superhighway and all too easily lure unsuspecting users. Identity theft is an issue, as is the loss of privacy due to the 'data mining' practices of social media companies. On-line platforms allow stalkers to find the addresses and phone numbers of unwary users who are bullied, shamed and harassed mercilessly.

The hundreds of millions of young users who were never intended to be on social media (SM) are most vulnerable to security breaches, sometimes with lethal consequences.

Net evangelists cheer the virtual world with little reservation. Yet while there's scant evidence that daily on-line engagement contributes to, say, character development in our young, we do have evidence of Net dependence and SM addiction, with negative impacts on personal well-being and productivity.

The SM crisis is hard to miss: If kids (the unintended users for whom the Net was not designed) aren't safe on social media, if they can't effectively avoid the worst of the Darkweb, we've got a social catastrophe - a growing challenge to physical and mental health. The opportunity, simply put, is this: If social media is reformed with systemic safety features, if parents and teachers put sensible limits on screen time and age restrictions on Net use, we just might make the best of a very tough situation: benefit from the Lightweb by minimising its shadow.

Resources for parents and kids:

- www.notforkids.info is a book for younger children to teach them how to respond if they see images online that make them feel uncomfortable.
- www.itstimewetalked.com.au has fact sheets about how to start a conversation about pornography and the damage it can do.

Safety tips for using social media:

Tell them what to do if they find themselves in a chatroom; how to respond if someone asks for a nude picture and how to end an uncomfortable text or e-mail conversation.

No matter how they're using them, here are a few things to keep in mind when they're being social on-line.

Don't use their real name:

It may seem obvious, but for many teens, it's not: Use an alias (a made-up name) for on sites such as MySpace. It's fine to tell trusted friends from school how to find their profile and what name you use for chatting and instant messaging, but keep their last name, age and other identifying information off their page if possible. It keeps a lot of shady characters from looking up other information about them, such as their address or what school they attend.

Be private:

Especially if they can't use an alias, they need to be extremely careful about who they let into their inner circle of friends on social networking sites. Consider setting their profile to private so they can carefully screen who can view their page.

Also, make sure they don't post photos that might give people the wrong idea about them. Here's a good rule of thumb: *If they'd be embarrassed for their favourite teacher or their best friend's parents to see it - it probably doesn't belong on their page.*

Keep their address and phone number to themselves:

Even if they screen their on-line friends carefully, it's good common sense to keep as much contact information to themselves as possible. They shouldn't share the name of their school or even their favourite after-school hangout on their page - even in a bulletin or invitation.

If they must list some contact information, list their secondary e-mail account, not the one they use for everyday stuff. Spammers and phishers love to grab e-mail addresses from Facebook and MySpace pages, so they should use an e-mail address with a good spam filter, too.

Set time limits:

Taking quizzes, writing comments and posting videos on their site or their friends' sites is a lot of fun, but it can easily eat up an entire afternoon. They need to set aside a specific amount of time - say, forty-five minutes to check their messages, send a few shout-outs and maybe play a quick game of Scrabulous.

If they're craving a chat, they need to ***make sure their homework is done*** and that they don't have family obligations before they hop on-line. Better yet, why not call their friend on the telephone or meet up with them to listen to music or watch their favourite TV show?

Be respectful:

Use the same sense of decency and etiquette that they would at school: i.e. they don't flirt with their friends' girlfriends and boyfriends; and apologise if they've hurt someone's feelings and avoid teasing, bullying or picking on others. The Internet has a karma all its own: What they dish out is going to make its way back to them; it's just a matter of time. (The same goes for kindness and good behaviour, of course.)

Your child isn't a little kid any more, and that means that by now, s/he should have mastered certain independence skills. Teens are capable of doing a lot, and learning how to master certain everyday skills will motivate your child to learn more and feel like a big kid.

Pornography:

Parents/teachers/schools need to give children basic information on smartphone and social media usage such as how to protect their password, ensure personal safety on-line, the dangers of sexting, what constitutes cyber-bullying and when sharing nude images can become a criminal offence. They need to point out that porn does not reflect a healthy relationship and is a distorted view of sex; is not a template for how they should conduct their own intimate lives; and can forever spoil their enjoyment of having a normal sexual relationship with their partner. Some males who have viewed pornography for years, find that they become impotent when trying to have normal sexual relations with a woman.

Conclusion:

Explain about kids being driven to suicide by cyber-bullying; those who now have a criminal record for sharing pornographic images and those hospitalised because they were on their phones when crossing the road.

Encourage your children to stay off social media and to use e-mails to interact on-line with their friends or have phone or in-person conversations. Adults as well need to know that they have to stay off social media to protect themselves from identity fraud, stalking and other crimes committed on social media.

'Just say NO' to using social media except to learn about companies, organisations, schools, community events, government bodies etc. Communicate instead with e-mails or phone to trusted friends and family.

Chapter 9
SCHOOL BULLYING

'Kids will be kids' or *'boys will be boys'* was often the response by adults when a child complained about bullying. We now know that bullying is actually assault and victims are protected by law when that happens. Bullies learn young that words can be used to hurt - so they experiment. They want to experience the feeling of power that comes with being able to manipulate someone. For some kids, it is something they try once. In others it becomes a way of life and every situation becomes a power struggle - with their parents, their teachers, their siblings and their playmates.

The bully does not have to be the nicest, best-looking or the funniest kid. S/he just has to know how to form a group and then take charge. They make the rules and decide whether they will play with a new kid or make his/her life miserable via bullying.

One daughter was caught shoplifting. The family was horrified, but were even more upset months later when the full story was revealed. The girl was stealing to avoid being attacked by a bully. She was ordered to steal, told what to steal and if she didn't bring the goods to school - she was in for it. The fact that the bully had so much control over the girl that she would take the chance of being arrested to avoid a bully, should tell us the power these bullies have over others.

Differences between child and adult bullying:

There are two main differences:

An adult is selected for bullying because they are good at their job and popular with people (the bully is a weak, inadequate individual who is driven by jealousy and envy). If there is a child in the class who is socially less popular than the rest, then this child is likely to be targeted by the bully. If no such obvious child exists, then the bully will pick on any child they think is unable or unwilling to fight. A key factor in the bully's choice is any child who is unwilling to resort to violence to resolve conflict - in other words, a child who has integrity and good moral codes. Given that bullies are driven by jealousy and envy, any child who is bright and popular is also likely to be targeted. Parents, teachers and carers must ensure that these children know how to deal with bullying.

Using fear:

Once bullying starts, many children will side with or appear to side with the bully because they know that otherwise they themselves might be bullied.

The school bully is a deeply unpopular child with whom other children associate, not through friendship, but through fear.

Many studies that show bullies to be popular fail to make this distinction. Also, the education system is biased towards physical strength (i.e. undue emphasis on sport and rewards for sporting achievement) while artistic achievements are undervalued. Children (and adults) who are bullied tend to be imaginative, creative, caring and responsible. Children (and adults) who bully are unimaginative, uncaring, aggressive, emotionally immature, inadequate (especially in social skills) and irresponsible.

There is a lot of anecdotal evidence to suggest that the child who learns to bully at school *and who gets away with it,* then goes on to be the serial bully in the workplace. The evidence suggests that the child who is bullied at school also goes on to be a likely target of bullying in the workplace.

This has nothing to do with being predisposed to being bullied - it has to do with the innate qualities of good people.

By the time a person enters adulthood at around the age of 18, their behaviour patterns are set and only time or a traumatic experience can alter these patterns. However, people who are likely to be bullied have a considerable learning capability and thus have a greater capacity to modify their behaviour as an adult. People who are bullies or prone to have limited learning capacity (especially in interpersonal and behavioural skills) will often exhibit bullying behaviours for the rest of their lives.

Emotionally, the bully remains a young child and their attention-seeking behaviour is characteristic of a two-year-old throwing a temper tantrum in order to gain attention. Serial bullies have psychopathic or sociopathic tendencies that include a learning blindness and an apparent lack of insight into their behaviour and its effect on others. The second major difference between adult and child bullying is that the child bully can be helped to develop better ways of behaving providing that:

- Everyone knows and understands what bullying is and why bullies bully;.
- Everyone knows and understands that bullying is unacceptable.
- Incidents of bullying are nipped in the bud.
- The bully is called to account in a firm, but kind and supportive manner *without* physical punishment (the child bully is usually deeply unhappy and has very low self-esteem).
- The bully is subsequently supervised and supported in learning more appropriate ways of interacting with other children.
- All children are taught how to be assertive;
- All children are taught how to spot bullying and intercede or report it;
- All children are empowered to help both target and bully.

This is where society needs to place its emphasis - on helping these children develop into better adults.

The child bully often (although not always) comes from a dysfunctional aggressive home environment where s/he is learning by example. Remember also that bullying (like abuse with which it is closely associated) is independent of class or financial status.

Bullying is one of the most underrated and enduring problems in school today and only about one incident in twenty-five is reported. It can leave deep psychological scars and even drive children to suicide. We hear more about bullies these days because the incidents are bloodier and the consequences more terrifying. No more is it just a bloodied nose or black eye at recess, now we hear of guns, knives, murders and suicides.

Something about the bullying we hear about these days feels different. It's not always the mean big kid beating up the scared little kid. It's often six or seven kids beating up one scared little kid. Or extorting lunch money, stealing jackets or six or seven girls 'swarming' and beating the girl who doesn't 'fit in.'

Bullying occurs on average every seven minutes and each bullying episode lasts about 37 seconds. Sixty per cent of children identified as bullies before they are eight years old, will have a criminal conviction by the age of twenty-four, so it's important that parents, teachers and the community do something to curb their bullying. If the bullies don't end up in jail, they'll end up involved in other violent behaviour like workplace bullying or spousal abuse.

According to a recent survey, bullying is not restricted to Western nations... some 94 per cent of Chinese students feel unsafe in school as the incidence of violence and bullying rise.

Case study:

Joe, who lives in Cape Breton, sent his son to the Sydney Academy. He had picked that school because of its zero-tolerance bullying policy - but the system let him down. When his teen-aged son told him that he wanted to kill himself rather than put up with any more bullying at school, he and his wife were shocked and devastated. They had missed the early signs, a change in attitude and behaviour - because their son was covering up. After comforting his son and wife - the father called the police and laid charges against the bully. Shortly after Joe and his family moved away from Cape Breton to a new and safer school environment.

What constitutes school bullying?

Most children joke around with each other, call each other games or rough-house - and yet these incidents are not normally called bullying. The difference lies in the relationship of the bully and the victim and the intent of that interaction. It normally occurs between individuals who are *not* friends. There's a power difference between the bully and the victim. The bully is usually bigger, tougher, physically stronger or has the ability to intimidate others.

Bullies and their victims come from all levels of socio-economic situations. Essentially they're looking for power that they're not getting or feeling anywhere else. Bullying is gender-neutral and can range from gang attacks to playground bullying. Researchers still can't explain why young girls act out their aggression in different ways from boys, but their biology is believed to be the main factor.

Girls use whispering campaigns and psychological bullying that their teachers find hard to detect. With girls, it mainly comes in the form of gossiping, spreading lies, backbiting, ruining reputations or social isolation that excludes one or more children from their group. Girls may be biologically hot-wired to engage in sophisticated, non-violent forms of aggression that can hurt just as much as a punch in the jaw from a boy. It's now believed that the non-physical conflict or indirect aggression is as dangerous to children as physical bullying.

When caught, many girls use tactics such as apologising or crying - that gets them out of trouble, but doesn't solve the underlying problem causing their bullying. Their targets feel that the bullying was directed towards excluding them from their peer group. Girls have different responses to authority than boys and in the way they deal with problems. They're more likely to skip school when problems arise. Many use truancy to deal with their bullies and often their teachers miss the real reason for their truancy. All truancy should be investigated to find the reasons behind the absence from school.

Boys tend to defend themselves and answer back, but can get themselves into worse trouble. Bullying amongst boys is usually physical and involves hitting and shoving.

Dysfunctional home environment:

For the child growing up in a dysfunctional or abusive home environment, bullying becomes a compulsive and obsessive behaviour. The bully has to have a target so s/he can displace his or her own aggression. The bullying child's parents may lack parental skills because they were brought up by parents who lacked appropriate behaviour skills and their parents were brought up in that same climate.

The cycle has to be broken. This is where schools can play a major role - **but only if they enforce anti-bullying policies and support the bullied child**. Helping parents adopt better parenting skills can also make a major difference if this is done tactfully.

Children who pick on other children could come from dysfunctional homes or homes with a lack of adult supervision. They could be victims of violence themselves, learning that violence is an acceptable way to interact with others or they could have missed a stage in their development and experienced a delay in their emotional development.

Bullies may have parents who ignored them or parents who have mothers who abused alcohol or drugs while they were pregnant. Violent television programs also reinforce that it's okay to act aggressively.

How long does bullying affect the target?

The memory of individual school yard bullying remains clear and unblemished for many adults long after they leave school. Any child or adult can tell you about a time s/he was bullied or s/he saw someone s/he knew being bullied. Bullies seek power. Bullying can be multiple episodes or consist of one single interaction. The intention of the bully is to cause the victim distress in some way.

Why are some children bullied?

When bullying is reported or violent incidents or suicide hit the headlines, the reason the child was bullied is often highlighted as a principal cause of the bullying.

Reasons for being picked on include being fat, thin, tall, short, hair or skin colour, being quiet, wearing glasses, having big ears, small ears, sticky-out ears, crooked teeth, being from a different culture, having different likes or dislikes, the 'wrong' clothes, unwillingness to use strength to defend him or herself or any perceived or fabricated 'excuse.' These excuses have one thing in common: ***they are all irrelevant!***

Each reason is a deceptive justification for the bully to indulge in a predictable pattern of violent (physical or psychological) behaviour against another child who is smaller, younger or less strong than the bully. The target is simply a useful object where the bully can displace his or her aggression. In other words, if a child is picked on because they are allegedly 'fat,' then losing weight will make no difference; the bully simply invents another justification. If children are bullied for their dinner money, then introducing cashless swipe cards will make no difference; the bullies invent other reasons.

Do not be deceived into thinking that the reason for bullying has any validity; it does not. Ignore it. Helping your child to lose weight or have cosmetic surgery or wear the 'in' fashions will make no difference. If you acknowledge the reason (i.e. telling overweight children to diet so they won't be bullied) you are unwittingly according the bully justification. Focus instead on why the bullying child needs to bully.

To tackle bullying you will have to liaise closely with the school and will probably have to talk to the bully's parents. Establish first of all whether this is an isolated incident (in which case nipping it in the bud is likely to have a high probability of success) or whether the child bully has a history of bullying behaviour. Remember that most children will try bullying at some time (including yours!) Most will realise that it's not an appropriate way of behaving and grow out of it quickly, especially if you help your child see why it's inappropriate and encourage and support them in learning better ways of behaving.

Ultimately, bullying is behaviour and behaviour is a choice. Therefore, bullying is a choice. While a poor home environment, poor parenting, poor role models etc. may be influencing factors in bullying, they are not a cause. Many children have poor home environments etc. but do not choose to bully; therefore these factors cannot be used as an excuse for bullying. It is the bully's choice to bully; a bad choice, but a choice.

Why aren't all children bullied? Most victims of bullying are approached early in their schooling or when they start a new school. Their first encounter with the bully usually determines whether the bully will approach them again. Children who are regularly victims of bullying tend to display 'vulnerable behaviours' when they react to their bully. Those behaviours in turn inspire the bully to continue with his or her attacks. Children who are more prone to be picked on by a bully often possess the following characteristics:

- Low self-esteem;
- Insecure;
- Lack social skills;
- Cry or become upset easily; and
- Have not learned the skills to defend or stand up for themselves.

Schools are a prime location for bullying. The majority of school bullying occurs in or close to school buildings. Many bullies try to pass off acts of aggression as roughhousing. The majority of victims don't report the bullying. Occasionally, a victim provokes the attack of their bully. These victims tease their bullies, making themselves a target by egging the bully on. These victims often don't know when to stop their provocation and usually aren't able to defend themselves when the balance of power shifts to the bully. Body language is everything when school bullies pick their prey.

Physical defects, like big ears, speech problems or a limp, don't normally play a role, but body language and level of self-esteem have everything to do with whether the child will or will not be bullied. Victims are encouraged to stand tall, say, 'No' in a loud voice and make eye contact. If victims are taught how to react, they can curb the problem. A bully needs an audience, but if witnesses simply leave the area when a situation happens or they report the bullying - the bullies lose their audience and have to account for their behaviour.

Only twenty-five per cent of students report that teachers intervene in bullying situations, while seventy-one per cent of teachers believe they always intervene.

Research shows us that the majority of students (60 per cent) have never been directly involved in any kind of bullying, as victims or as bullies (Psychology Today, September 1996). That said - most students have witnessed bullying incidents at the schoolyard. The unfortunate thing is they do nothing to stop the bullying!

Bullies are often socially accepted until their mid-teens. Despite their aggressive behaviour, they can even enjoy social popularity with their peers. But, by late adolescence, the bully's popularity begins to fade. Bullies lose their popularity as they get older and are eventually disliked by the majority of students. The paths of the mid-teen bully and his or her former victim rarely cross. By that age, teens have clearly defined their social set. Tragically, the bully finds him or herself becoming more excluded by his or her peers and often seeks alliances with gangs of other isolated individuals. These teen gangs often get into serious trouble with the law and others.

By senior high school, most regular bullying incidents are a thing of the past, but the memories of their abuse haunts victims and they continue to avoid their bully. Some carry their emotional scars for a lifetime.

Sixty percent of people who are identified as childhood bullies have at least one criminal conviction by the age of twenty-four. Those who carry their bullying behaviour with them into adulthood often develop a roster of problems: alcoholism, anti-social personality disorders and mental health disorders. If their behaviour is not treated, the bullies can grow up to bully their spouses, children and co-workers. Bullying becomes a habit, an easy method for the bullies to get what they want.

The children who manage to ward off the bully tend to have better social and conflict management skills. So this is where parents and teachers should place their emphasis in teaching children interpersonal skills. These children are better able to assert themselves without becoming aggressive or confrontational. Instead, they work out compromises and devise alternative solutions. These children appear to be more aware of people's feelings (empathetic skills) and are the children who can be most helpful in resolving disputes and assisting other children to get help.

Children who have been repeatedly victimised by a bully show certain behaviours and attitudes. Sometimes these behaviours are inconsistent with the child's typical behaviour. Many children are too embarrassed and humiliated to report victimisation and worry that speaking out will lead to more abuse.

Profiles of bullies and targets

Bullies:

Aggressive, physically strong; easily and willingly resorts to violence; poor communication skills; poor social skills; low self-esteem; insecure; may have a dysfunctional home life; thrives on control and dominance; thinks it's fun to torment and hurt children who are less physically strong; cowardly; exhibits attention-seeking behaviour and needs to be respected but can't distinguish between 'respect' and 'fear;' needs to impress; disrespectful and often contemptuous of others (both children and adults); emotionally and behaviourally immature; jealous and envious; divisive and dysfunctional; disruptive; academically below average; often lies; cannot and will not accept responsibility; uncaring; lacks empathy and exploitative.

Targets:

Physically not as strong as the bully; have a very low propensity to violence and will do everything to avoid resorting to violence to resolve conflict; are artistic; imaginative; creative; academically above average; different (although this is a relative term); caring and empathic; easily forgiving; high integrity; high moral standard; unwilling to resort to lying and deception; often independent; self-reliant; have good relationships with adults; not powerful and stays away from classroom politics.

Some people use the words 'swot,' 'isolated' and 'loner' to describe targets. I believe these have negative connotations that reinforce notions of 'victim type.' I prefer the words 'academically high performers and achievers,' 'tend to be independent rather than socialites' and 'often prefers to work alone and have no need to impress others.'

I also prefer the word 'target' to 'victim.' The word 'victim' allows bullies and their supporters to tap into and stimulate people's preconceived notions and prejudices of 'victimhood,' i.e.: that victims are 'weak' and somehow bring the bullying upon themselves. 'Target,' on the other hand, correctly highlights the deliberate act of choice and selection by the bully.

While it is often the target that is regarded as 'weak and inadequate,' it is always the bully who is weak and inadequate - as evidenced by the need to bully. People of strong character and high integrity don't need to bully.

Facts from **'Take Action Against Bullying'** *a manual developed by three Coquitlam, British Columbia, Canada teachers for use in schools or by parents:*

There are four kinds of bullies:

Physical bullies:

The least sophisticated type of bully. Action-oriented, will hit or kick victims or will take or damage their property. This is the least sophisticated type of bullying because it is so easy to identify. Physical Bullies are soon known to the entire population in the school. As they get older, their attacks usually become more aggressive. These aggressive characteristics manifest themselves as bullies become adults.

Verbal bullies:

Use words to hurt or humiliate another person. This includes name-calling, insulting, making racist comments and constant teasing. This type of bullying is the easiest to inflict on other children. It is quick and to the point. It can occur in the least amount of time available and its effects can be more devastating in some ways than physical bullying because there are no visible scars.

Relational bullies:

They try to convince their peers to exclude or reject a certain person or people and cut the victims off from their social connections. This type of bullying is linked to verbal bullying and usually occurs when children (most often girls) spread nasty rumours about others or exclude an ex-friend from the peer group. The most devastating effect with this type of bullying is the rejection by the peer group at a time when children most need their social connections.

Reactive bullies:

They straddle a fence of being a bully and/or victim. They are often the most difficult to identify because at first glance, they seem to be targets for other bullies. However, reactive bullies often taunt bullies and bully other people themselves. Most of the incidents are physical in nature. These victims are impulsive and react quickly to intentional and unintentional physical encounters. In some cases, reactive victims begin as victims and become bullies as they try to retaliate. A reactive victim will approach a person who has been bullying him/her and say something like, *'You better not bug me today, otherwise I'll tell the teacher and boy, will you be in trouble and so you just better watch out.'*

Statements such as this are akin to waving a red flag in front of a raging bull and may provoke a bully into action. They then fight back and claim self-defence.

Sexual Harassment

Very few records have been kept about the number of children who have been sexually harassed at school, but sexual harassment in school is no different than sexual harassment in the workplace. One sexual harassment code states that sexual harassment can include one or more of the following:

- Unwelcome sexual remarks such as jokes, innuendoes, teasing and verbal abuse;
- Taunts about a person's body, attire, age, sexual preference, family situation;
- Displays of pornographic, offensive or derogatory pictures;
- Offensive e-mails or texts;
- Cyber-bullying;
- Practical jokes that cause awkwardness or embarrassment;
- Unwelcome invitations or requests, whether indirect or explicit;
- Intimidation;
- Leering or suggestive gestures;
- Condescension or paternalistic treatment that undermines self-respect;
- Unnecessary physical contact such as touching, patting, pinching, punching or physical assault.

Schools need to include sexual harassment in their anti-bullying policies. Students must understand that sexual comments (including those relating to sexual preference) are not permitted and are a form of bullying. Students and witnesses to sexual harassment would deal with it the same way they would deal with bullying incidents.

Students should also be aware that complaints can be made to their applicable Human Rights Commission or Equal Rights Commission if a school fails in their duty of care and does not stop the behaviour. One sexual harassment law states that:

> *'Any person responsible for any act of sexual harassment, any supervisor, manager or person in a position of authority (teacher or principal) who is aware of the sexual harassment and does not take immediate and appropriate action (as well as the company) will be named in any complaint brought before the Human Rights Commission.'*

This means that teachers and school authorities can no longer 'look the other way' and pretend that sexual harassment is not occurring. They must step in and stop the harassment; otherwise they too could be charged with sexual harassment because it would appear that they condoned the behaviour.

Types of pupil bullying

Physical aggression:

This behaviour is more common among boys than girls. It includes pushing, shoving, punching, kicking, poking and tripping people. It may also take the form of severe physical assault. While boys commonly engage in 'mess fights,' they can often be used as a disguise for physical harassment or inflicting pain.

Damage to property:

Personal property can be the focus of attention for the bully: this may result in damage to clothing, school books and other learning material or interference with a pupil's locker or bicycle. The contents of school bags and pencil cases may be scattered on the floor. Items of personal property may be defaced, broken, stolen or hidden.

Extortion:

Demands for money may be made, often accompanied by threats (sometimes carried out) in the event of the victim not promptly 'paying up.' Victims' lunches, lunch vouchers or lunch money may be taken. Victims may also be forced into theft of property for delivery to the bully. Sometimes, this tactic is used with the sole purpose of incriminating the victim.

Intimidation:

Some bullying behaviour takes the form of intimidation; it is based on the use of very aggressive body language with the voice being used as a weapon. Particularly upsetting to victims can be the so-called 'look' - a facial expression that conveys aggression and/or dislike.

Abusive Telephone Calls, texts or e-mails:

The abusive anonymous messages are a form of intimidation or bullying. The anonymous contact is very prevalent where teachers are the victims of bullying.

Isolation:

This form of bullying behaviour seems to be more prevalent among girls. A certain person is deliberately isolated, excluded or ignored by some or the entire class group. This practice is usually initiated by the person engaged in bullying behaviour. It may be accompanied by writing insulting remarks about the victim on blackboards or in public places, by passing around notes about or drawings of the victim or by whispering insults about them loud enough to be heard.

Name Calling:

Persistent name-calling directed at the same individual(s) which hurts, insults or humiliates, should be regarded as a form of bullying behaviour. Most name-calling of this type refers to physical appearance, e.g. 'big ears,' size or clothes worn.

Accent or distinctive voice characteristics may attract negative attention. Academic ability can also provoke name-calling. This tends to operate at two extremes; first, there are those who are singled out for attention because they are perceived to be slow or weak academically. These pupils are often referred to as 'dummies,' 'dopes' or 'donkeys.' At the other extreme are those who, because they are perceived as high achievers, are labelled 'swots,' 'brain-boxes,' 'licks,' 'teachers' pets,' etc.

Teasing:

This behaviour usually refers to the good-natured banter that goes on as part of the normal social interchange between people. However, when this teasing extends to very personal remarks aimed again and again at the one individual about appearance, clothing, personal hygiene or involves references of an uncomplimentary nature to members of one's family, particularly if couched in sexual innuendo, then it assumes the form of bullying. It may take the form of suggestive remarks about a pupil's sexual orientation.

Effects of Bullying

Pupils who are being bullied may develop feelings of insecurity and extreme anxiety and thus may become more vulnerable. Self-confidence may be damaged with a consequent lowering of their self-esteem. While they may not talk about what is happening to them, their suffering is indicated through changes in mood and behaviour. Bullying may occasionally result in suicide. It is therefore important to be alert to changes in behaviour as early intervention is desirable.

Why don't other students help the victim?

They're reluctant to report bullying because they fear retaliation from the bully themselves. Children who are not bullies or victims have a powerful role to play in shaping the behaviour of other children. It's the 60 per cent of children within a school who are not bullied or victimised who hold the key to stop bullying. Children need to be encouraged to speak up on behalf of children they see being bullied. Students who witness bullying have the potential to reduce bullying by refusing to watch bullying, reporting bullying incidents and/or distracting the bully. The key to a successful anti-bullying campaign is to involve everyone in working toward a solution.

The bullying cycle works on witnesses as follows:

- They fear that teachers will confront the bully in such a way that the witnesses are now at risk.
- They fear that their confidentiality will be breached and/or their status within their peer group will be compromised.

Bullies survive by creating the myth that if their behaviour is reported, they will retaliate swiftly and severely. This threat paralyses the victims and witnesses into a code of silence that allows the bully to extend his/her reign of terror.

Unfortunately, many teachers and school staff don't know how to intervene properly, so the bullying continues. This leads to more helplessness for the victims and gives more power to the bullies who know they will get away with their bullying and/or feel the school has condoned their behaviour.

Teachers need to make it safe for their students to report any bullying incident. They accomplish this by respecting the anonymity of the victim and witnesses. Until the victims and witnesses trust that this will happen - bullying will go unreported and bullies will be encouraged to continue their actions. Bullies must know the consequences for bullying and schools must consistently enforce the rules.

Bullies need counselling so they can learn how to behave in a socially acceptable manner, as their victims need to learn assertiveness and have confidence that any reported bullying will be dealt with swiftly and effectively by authority figures.

As parents:

As soon as their children begin to interact with others, parents need to teach them not to be bullies and how not to be bullied. Teach children the proper words so they can express their feelings. If their pre-schoolers start calling others names or use unkind words, both parents must intervene immediately and consistently. If they hear comments such as, *'He's not my friend, so he can't share my toys'* the parent must respond with, *'I expect you to share your toys.'* Many parents do not know how to intervene in bullying situations, so they overlook the bullying.

Parents need to ask their children if they are being bullied. Whether the child seems to be bullied or not, they should ask them:

- *'Has anyone bullied you - either going to school or at school? Bullying is different from having fights with your friends, because although fights are unpleasant, they are not as serious.'*
- *'If you have been bullied or seen someone else bullied, have you reported it?'*
- *'Is it still ongoing?'*
- *'Why did you not report it to your teacher or at least to us?'*

Then follow through with school authorities and don't relent until the bullying has stopped. If the school doesn't have an anti-bullying policy, ask why they don't. Insist that they write and enforce one or move your child to another school.

Many parents don't know their children are being bullied until it's too late. Most bullied children show signs - a lack of vitality, either depression or withdrawal, may be afraid to go to school or come home missing supplies or possessions. It's a tough call for parents and teachers to make.

When is bullying dangerous and when is it child's play? Parents need to keep their eyes and ears open. If a beloved DVD player disappears - find out where it went. If money starts disappearing - find out where it's going. If a child is upset after a phone call - s/he's giving you a clue. Follow it. The parents of a loner need to do all they can to help their child find that one true friend, because together, they can more successfully fend off bullies.

A child's first interaction with a bully will determine whether that child will be victimised. Body language and level of self-esteem have everything to do with who will be chosen as a target. Bullies pick their prey by first observing the target's body language. Kids need strategies for controlling their body language and dealing with difficult people, just as adults do.

This is why parents need to instruct their children about what constitutes bullying and insist that they are told immediately if they see or are involved in bullying. It's vital that parents continue the dialogue and they should take the bullying seriously. If they let it go and don't address it - the problem will get bigger.

Is your child a bully?

Here are some signs that your child might be a bully:

- Complaints from school about your child's behaviour;
- Complaints from other parents about your child's behaviour;
- Seems to have unaccountable money;
- Buys things that you know s/he can't afford;
- Explanations that their friends gave them the designer clothes they're wearing;
- Have a cocky, superior air about them.

Is your child a target?

Here are some signs that your child might be a target:

- Has trouble sleeping or has lost his/her appetite;

- Crying, depression, sudden rages;
- Is reluctant to go to school - gives excuses that s/he is ill (when you doubt if s/he is);
- Has been in physical fights;
- Comes home from school overly hungry;
- Comes home from school with books or clothing torn;
- Asks you to drive him/her to school or changes his/her route to school;
- 'Loses' things - a sign that someone is stealing the child's items.

Signs and symptoms of bullying behaviour:

The following signs/symptoms may suggest that a pupil is being bullied:

- Anxiety about travelling to and from school;
- Requesting parents to drive or collect them;
- Changing route of travel;
- Avoiding regular times for travelling to and from school;
- Unwillingness to go to school;
- Refusal to attend;
- Deterioration in educational performance;
- Loss of concentration;
- Loss of enthusiasm and interest in school;
- Pattern of physical illnesses (e.g. headaches, stomach aches);
- Possessions missing or damaged;
- Spontaneous out-of-character comments about either pupils or teachers;

- Increased requests for money or stealing money;
- Unexplained changes either in mood or behaviour (it may be particularly noticeable before returning to school after weekends or more specifically after longer school holidays);
- Visible signs of anxiety or distress – stammering, withdrawing, nightmares, difficulty in sleeping, crying, not eating, vomiting, bedwetting;
- Unexplained bruising or cuts or damaged clothing;
- Reluctance and/or refusal to say what is troubling him/her.

Those signs do not necessarily mean that a pupil is being bullied. If repeated or occurring in combination, those signs do warrant investigation in order to establish what is affecting the pupil.

School Hazing

Years ago, it was common to have hazing of junior students at the beginning of a school year. Most of the pranks revolved around being the servant of an older student for a day, but lately, that hazing has taken a dangerous turn and students have been seriously hurt, maimed or even killed when pranks went amiss.

One Canadian student almost died when the senior students forced their 'slaves' to consume raw alcohol. One boy was forced to drink a half bottle of vodka until he passed out. When students couldn't revive him, they called for an ambulance. The boy barely survived the ordeal.

Bullying of school personnel:

Bullying of school personnel by means of physical assault, damage to property, verbal abuse, threats to people's families etc.

Teacher behaviour:

A teacher may, unwittingly or otherwise, engage in, instigate or reinforce bullying behaviour in a number of ways:

- Using sarcasm or other insulting or demanding form of language when addressing pupils;
- Making negative comments about a pupil's appearance or background;
- Humiliating directly or indirectly, a pupil who is particularly academically weak or outstanding or vulnerable in other ways;
- Using any gesture or expression of a threatening or intimidatory nature or any form of degrading physical contact or exercise.

Preventing school bullying:

Our children are constantly exposed to violence - and I don't just mean watching gun battles and murder scenes on the television. Have you really paid attention to what they're watching in our sports-addicted society? If you have, you'll notice how much aggression and violence is now used in the name of 'sport.' Grown men poke other players, gouge bodies and generally act the part of the school bully. And we wonder why our children clone that behaviour!

Our society needs to look seriously at cleaning up the violence we now see in several of our sports. Sport used to be 'sportsmanlike' but the violent actions we see in our football players - can not be called sporting at all. The AFL and Aussie Rules administratiuon staff should look at the image they are giving to young Australian supporters. This is not sportsmanship - it's bullying and sets a terrible example for the impressionasble youngsters of Australia. They should be ashamed of themselves.

Schools <u>must</u> deal quickly and effectively with any bullying or unsportsmanlike behaviour displayed during sporting activities, whether it's from the players, the coaches or from their audience. Often their parents can display very aggressive behaviour and encourage the same in their children.

Comprehensive supervision and monitoring measures through which all areas of school activity are kept under observation. It is important and indeed, it is the responsibility of the school authority in conjunction with staff and pupils to develop a system under which proper supervisory and monitoring measures are in place to deal with incidents of bullying behaviour. Such measures might include control of school activities on a rota basis. All pupils but, in particular, senior pupils can be seen as a resource to assist in countering bullying.

School councils, where applicable, and other school clubs and societies may also be of assistance. It would, of course, be most desirable that non-teaching staff be part of the process in measures to counter bullying behaviour in schools. Also schemes need to be developed to involve all parents/guardians.

Procedures for reporting bullying behaviour

School authorities should ensure that there is a procedure for formal noting and reporting an incident of bullying behaviour and that such a procedure should be seen to be an integral part of the Code of Behaviour and Discipline in the school. This system should also provide for early detection of signs of indiscipline and/or significant change in mood or behaviour of pupils.

All reports of bullying (no matter how trivial) should be noted, investigated and dealt with by teachers. In that way pupils will gain confidence in 'telling.' This confidence factor is of vital importance. Serious cases of bullying behaviour by pupils should be referred immediately to the Principal or Vice-Principal.

Parents or guardians of victims and bullies should be informed by the Principal or Vice-Principal earlier rather than later of incidents so that they are given the opportunity of discussing the matter. They are then in a position to help and support their children before a crisis occurs.

Parents or guardians must be informed of the appropriate person to whom they can make their enquiries regarding incidents of bullying behaviour that they might suspect or that have come to their attention through their children or other parents/guardians.

It should be made clear to all pupils that when they report incidents of bullying that they are not telling tales, but are behaving responsibly. Individual teachers in consultation with the appropriate staff member should record and take appropriate measure regarding reports of bullying behaviour in accordance with the school's policy and Code of Behaviour and Discipline.

Non-teaching staff such as secretaries, caretakers, cleaners should be encouraged to report any incidents of bullying behaviour witnessed by them or mentioned to them, to the appropriate teaching member of staff.

In the case of a complaint regarding a staff member, this should normally in the first instance be raised with the staff member in question and if necessary, with the Principal.

Where cases, relating to either a pupil or a teacher unresolved at school level, the matter should be referred to the School's Board of Management. If not solved at the Board level, refer to local Inspectorate.

Procedures for dealing with bullying behaviour:

Teachers are best advised to take a calm, unemotional problem-solving approach when dealing with incidents of bullying behaviour reported by pupils, staff, parents and guardians. Such incidents are best investigated outside the classroom situation to avoid the public humiliation of the victim or the pupil engaged in bullying, in an attempt to get both sides of the story. All interviews should be conducted with sensitivity and with due regard to the rights of all pupils concerned. Pupils who are not directly involved, but witnessed the event, can also provide very useful information in this way.

When analysing incidents of bullying behaviour, seek answers to questions of what, where, when, who and why. This should be done in a calm manner, setting an example in dealing effectively with a conflict in a non-aggressive manner.

If a gang is involved, each member should be interviewed individually and then the gang should be met as a group. Each member should be asked for his/her account of what happened to ensure that everyone is clear about what everyone else has said.

If it is concluded that a pupil has been engaged in bullying behaviour, it should be made clear to him/her how s/he is in breach of the Code of Behaviour and Discipline and try to get him/her to see the situation from the victim's point of view.

Each member of the gang should be helped to handle the possible pressures that often face them from the other members after interview by the teacher.

Teachers who are investigating cases of bullying behaviour should keep a written record of their discussions with those involved. It may also be appropriate or helpful to ask those involved to write down their account of the incidentor recorded the interview.

In cases where it has been determined that bullying behaviour has occurred; meet with the parents or guardians of the two parties involved as appropriate. Explain the actions being taken and the reasons for them, referring them to the school policy. Discuss ways in which they can reinforce or support the actions taken by the school.

Arrange for separate follow-up meetings with the two parties involved with a view to possibly bringing them together at a later date if the victim is ready and agreeable. This can have a therapeutic effect.

Program to deal with victims, bullies and their peers:

Pupils involved in bullying behaviour need assistance on an ongoing basis. For those low in self-esteem, opportunities should be developed to increase feelings of self-worth. Pupils who engage in bullying behaviour may need counselling to help them learn other ways of meeting their needs without violating the rights of others. Victims may need counselling and opportunities to participate in activities designed to raise their self-esteem and to develop their friendship and social skills whenever this is needed.

Research indicates that pupils identified as low achievers academically tend to be more frequently involved in bullying behaviour. It is, therefore, important that the learning strategies applied within the school allow for the enhancement of the pupil's self-worth. Pupils who observe incidents of bullying behaviour should be encouraged to discuss them with teachers.

Schools would work with and through the various local agencies to deal with all forms of bullying. There should be a whole-community approach to the problem of bullying behaviour. The school as a community is made up of management, teachers, non-teaching staff, pupils and parents/guardians. However, incidents of bullying behaviour extend beyond the school. It is known that they can occur on the journey to and from school. It is necessary, therefore, for anti-bullying school policy to embrace, as appropriate, those members of the wider school community who come directly in daily contact with school pupils.

For example, school bus drivers, school traffic wardens and local shopkeepers could be encouraged to play a positive role in assisting schools to counter bullying behaviour by reporting such behaviour to parents and/or schools as appropriate. Through such approaches, a network is formed.

In certain cases, however, it may be necessary to invite the assistance of other local persons and formal agencies such as general medical practitioners, health boards and their social workers and community workers.

A positive community attitude and involvement can, therefore, assist considerably in countering bullying behaviour in schools. The promotion of relevant home/school/community links is important for all schools in regard to countering bullying behaviour and should be encouraged as a normal part of the school's effective operation.

Evaluation of school bullying policies:

As part of the evaluation of the effectiveness of school policy on preventing and dealing with bullying, a programme of support for those pupils involved in bullying behaviour should be an integral part of the school's intervention process. It is advisable to monitor the effectiveness of school policy on this issue. Random surveys could be held to ascertain the level and type of bullying behaviour in school.

A school's anti-bullying code should be subject to continuous review in light of incidents of bullying behaviour. It could be included as an item on the agenda for school staff meetings.

Summary:

It's evident that bullying is a matter of increasing concern in our schools. It poses very real difficulties, therefore, for school behaviour and discipline. Because of this, it's essential that primary and post-primary schools adopt a policy aimed at countering the problem. This school policy should be drawn up after consultation with all the interested parties, i.e., teaching and non-teaching staff, pupils and parents/guardians.

It's necessary that the school policy should have general acceptance by the partners in the education of the pupils. In that way, it can be effective both from the point-of-view of preventing as well as dealing with bullying behaviour. An understanding of the factors that give rise to bullying is needed as well as sympathetic treatment of all those involved in the bullying behaviour. Furthermore, having regard to the nature of the problem, it must in certain circumstances, receive the attention of others directly outside of the school community.

In conclusion, the inclusion of a module on bullying behaviour in the pre-service training of teachers would be a positive step in alerting potential teachers to the problems caused by such behaviour in schools. Also, it is considered that the expansion of in-service courses to teachers on aspects of bullying behaviour would be of considerable benefit to the teaching profession in the process of raising awareness and developing techniques to deal with such behaviour.

Selecting a school:

When selecting a school for your child, avoid any school where there is no anti-bullying policy and especially where the staff or head claims, *'We don't need an anti-bullying policy. There's no bullying here.'*

It's in these schools that bullying is most prevalent!

If the school has an anti-bullying policy, check that it's effective. The first place to start is by ensuring that the school has an anti-bullying policy that is not only in place - but is enforced. These policies should not only include child bullies, but bullying that involves teachers, school staff and school principals. I believe that the federal government must set a standard for these policies and insist that every school abide by that standard. Laws must be put into place where serious physical and mental bullying by students would be penalised with fines and jail sentences. Some schools have a policy that is simply window-dressing and are not enforced.

A policy is only words on paper. Its effectiveness is in the commitment of all school staff to see that it's enforced. Talk to the pupils and ex-pupils in private and in confidence. Talk to the children who are artistic, gifted, of high integrity and non-aggressive - these are the ones most likely to be targeted by bullies.

To find out what a school is really like, ask for the following figures for the last academic year:

Presence of an anti-bullying policy:

- Does that policy include sexual harassment and school hazing?
- What proof is there that they follow that policy?
- Number of student complaints about bullying actions and how did they deal with them;
- Number of expelled students and reasons why they were expelled;
- Number of suicides and attempted suicides amongst pupils;
- Number of suspensions of staff;
- Number of dismissals of staff;
- Number of times the school is involved in employment tribunals or legal action against employees;
- Amount of damage of school property including graffiti.

When judging which school is likely to be best for your child, don't be fooled by league tables; these show only exam results (called 'standards' by OFSTED and the DfEE) which are only one aspect of school life. Remember that academic exam results are one of the least reliable indicators of potential and that many of the world's most successful people (i.e. Albert Einstein [physics], Soichira Honda [Honda Motor Corporation], Ray Kroc [founder of MacDonalds]) left school with few or no qualifications.

To find out what a school is really like, ask for the following figures for the last academic year:

- Number of:
    - days when supply staff are engaged;
    - different supply staff engaged;
    - stress breakdowns of staff;
    - suicides and attempted suicides amongst staff;
    - suicides and attempted suicides amongst pupils;
    - ill-health retirements;
    - early retirements;
    - grievances started;
    - uses of disciplinary procedures (verbal and written warnings issued);
    - suspensions of staff;
    - dismissals of staff;
    - times the employer is involved in employment tribunals or legal action against employees;
    - pupil exclusions;
- Attendance record of pupils;
- Rate of staff turnover;
- Amount of staff sick leave;
- Amount of damage to school property including graffiti;
- Presence of an anti-bullying policy;

- Views of the pupils, especially past pupils.

The figures will also give you a good indication to how wisely your council tax and other taxes are being spent. Bullying prevents all children in the class from undertaking their studies; exam results will be lower than they could and should be.

School bullying must stop! This won't happen until society, education departments and the courts implement and enforce zero-tolerance policies relating to school bullying.

Because bullies are driven by jealousy and envy, any child who is bright and popular is likely to be targeted by bullies. Parents, teachers and carers must ensure that these children are prepared to deal with bullying.

Recommendations:

Here are my recommendations that should result in a lower level of school bullying:

- All countries should make school bullying seriously by making *laws* to protect children that would be similar to the Act in place in the *State of New Jersey Anti-bullying Legislation* (see pages 182 – 185 of this Act). No Code of Conduct or Guidance Notes will be as effective – it must be legislation.

- Federal Education Departments of each country would set up and enforce anti-bullying school policies to ensure all students are protected consistently - no matter where they live in a country.

- Ensure that every school has an anti-bullying policy that is not only in place - but is enforced.

- Provide more involvement by community groups to counsel both targets and bullies to find out what is behind the bullying.

- More parental involvement with the schools via parent-teacher associations.
- More police influence in schools where required.
- Severe punishment or monetary fines for repeat offenders.
- Targets of bullying would be shown how to act more assertively.
- Children would be encouraged to speak up on behalf of children they witnessed being bullied.
- Bullies would know the consequences for bullying and schools would consistently enforce the rules.
- Bullies would obtain counselling so they could learn how to behave in a socially acceptable manner.
- Targets need to have confidence that any reported bullying would be dealt with swiftly and effectively by authority figures.
- Teachers would make it safe for their students to report any bullying incident by respecting the anonymity of the victim and witnesses.

Until those issues are resolved, parents must be very selective in choosing their children's schools. They will avoid schools that lack anti-bullying policies and will be especially wary of staff that insist they have no bullying in their schools. It's these schools that have the worst bullying records. If the school does have an anti-bullying policy, make sure it's a good one that is not only effective - but is enforced. The key to a successful anti-bullying campaign is to involve everyone in the community so we need your help to make it happen!

Unless your child's school fills those criteria – 'Just say NO' and look elsewhere for a school that will provide a zero-bullying environment.

Chapter 10
Cyber Bullying:

What is Cyber bullying?

Cyber bullying is any harassment that occurs via the Internet. Vicious forum posts, name-calling in chat rooms, posting fake profiles on web sites and mean or cruel e-mail messages are all ways of cyber bullying.

Cyber bullying is threatening, lying about, stalking or otherwise harassing a person on-line or via other electronic communication devices like a cell phone. It is becoming a bigger problem as more and more people spend time on the Internet. There are several behaviours that are considered cyber bullying, including:

- Sending harassing messages;
- Impersonating another person and gaining trust;
- Posting someone else's personal information;
- Posting false or unsavoury information about another person;
- Posting private or doctored pictures about another person;
- Using the Internet to encourage others to bully the target.

Cyber Bullies (and other bullies such as school and workplace bullies) use these behaviours:

- They are vicious, criticising and vindictive in private - but charming in front of witnesses. (Others often don't see this side of their nature).
- Are very controlling of others. If someone resists, they're vicious in their attack to regain that control.
- They don't listen to others, lack conscience, show no remorse, are drawn to power, are emotionally cold and

flat, dysfunctional, disruptive, divisive, rigid and inflexible, selfish, insincere, insecure, immature and lack interpersonal skills.

- Are charming and convincing, which they use to make up for their lack of empathy.
- Are very convincing or compulsive liars and when called upon, can fabricate authentic-sounding reasons for their behaviour.
- Hiding under their charming exterior is often sexual harassment, discrimination and racial prejudice.
- On the surface, they seem very self-assured, but inside they're very insecure people.
- They excel at deception - have vivid imaginations - are often very creative.
- They encourage feelings of shame, embarrassment, guilt and fear - for that is how all abusers, including child sex abusers, control and silence their targets;
- When others describe their uncaring nature, they respond with impatience, irritability and aggression.
- Often have an overwhelming, unhealthy and narcissistic need to portray themselves as being a wonderful, kind, caring and compassionate person; in contrast to their behaviour and treatment of others.
- Are oblivious to the discrepancy between how they like to be seen (and believe they are seen) and how they are actually seen.
- Are unaware of the difference between having leadership qualities (maturity, decisiveness, assertiveness, trust and integrity) and bullying (immaturity, impulsiveness, aggression, distrust and deceitfulness).
- Show inappropriate attitudes to sexual matters or behaviour.

- Refuse to acknowledge, value or praise others.
- When called upon to account for their actions, they aggressively deny everything and then counter-attack with distorted or fabricated criticism and allegations. If this is insufficient, they quickly feign being the target, often bursting into tears (the purpose is to avoid answering the question and thus evade accountability by manipulating others using guilt).

Who are the targets of the cyber bullies?

It's often assumed that targets of bullying are weak and inadequate. Targets of bullying are assumed to be loners, but most are independent, self-reliant and have no need for gangs or cliques. They have neither a need to impress nor are they interested in putting others down.

Bullies select individuals who prefer to use dialogue to resolve conflict and who will go to great lengths to avoid conflict. The targets constantly try to use negotiation rather than resorting to grievance and legal action. Targets are chosen because they're competent and popular. Bullies are jealous of the easy and stable relationships targets have with others.

A key factor in the bully's choice is any individual who is unwilling to resort to violence to resolve conflict - in other words, a person who has integrity and good moral codes. Given that bullies are driven by jealousy and envy, anyone who is bright and popular is also likely to be targeted.

Parents, teachers and carers must ensure that these children know how to deal with bullying. Once bullying starts, many children will side with, or appear to side with the bully because they know that otherwise they themselves will be bullied.

> *The bully is a deeply unpopular child with whom other children associate, not through friendship, but through fear.*

Many studies that show bullies to be popular, fail to make this distinction. Also, the education system is biased towards physical strength (i.e.: undue emphasis on sport and rewards for sporting achievement) while artistic achievements are undervalued. Children who are bullied tend to be imaginative, creative, caring and responsible. Children who bully are unimaginative, uncaring, aggressive, emotionally immature, inadequate (especially in social skills) and irresponsible.

What are the results to the target of bullying?

- The targets' constant high stress level interferes with their immune system causing frequent illnesses such as the flu, ulcers, irritable bowel problems, skin problems such as eczema, psoriasis, athlete's foot, shingles, colds, coughs, ear, nose and throat infections.
- They suffer from aches and pains in the joints and muscles or have back pain with no obvious cause that won't go away or respond to treatment.
- They're disempowered such that they become dependent on the bully to allow them to get through each day without their life being made a hell.
- Initially they're reluctant to act against their bullies and report them knowing that they could accelerate the abuse. Later this gives way to a strong urge to act against the bullies so that others don't have to suffer a similar fate.
- In the workplace, many targets are so traumatised by the bullying that they need professional help or take stress leave until the incidence of bullying is investigated. Bullies love this because they can claim that their target is "mentally ill" or "mentally unstable" or has a "mental health problem." It's much more likely that this allegation is a projection of the bully's own mental health problems which have not been treated.
- Their bodies' batteries never have an opportunity to recharge.

- For the targets that become victims of abuse, their world and self-view is shattered and they may find it impossible to function normally or effectively. Research would indicate that often those who suffer most from unacceptable abusive behaviour are those with the most to give - those with high expectations of themselves and those who are prepared to go the extra mile because they believe that what they do is meaningful and important.

The targets' behaviour:

- An overwhelming desire for acknowledgement, understanding, recognition and validation of their experience and strong motivation for justice to be done.
- An unwillingness to talk or interact with the bully.
- An unusually strong sense of vulnerability, victimisation or persecution.
- An unusually strong desire to educate the public and help the public introduce bullying prevention laws.
- An overwhelming sense of betrayal and an inability or unwillingness to trust anyone.
- Headaches and migraines.
- Shattered self-confidence and low self-esteem;
- Became seriously depressed, especially upon waking.
- Became tired, exhausted and lethargic.
- Found their levels of guilt were abnormally high which precluded them from starting new relationships.
- Found themselves constantly fatigued (like Chronic Fatigue Syndrome) or sweated, trembled, shook or had heart palpitations.
- Often been highly upset by the amount of anger they felt towards their abuser and were horrified by the mental pictures of creative, cruel, torturous ways they could pay back their abuser.

- Suffered from panic attacks triggered by any reminder of the experience.
- Impaired memory that was due to suppressing horrific memories.
- Physical numbness (toes, fingertips, lips) and emotional numbness (especially the inability to feel joy).
- Constantly been on alert because their fight or flight mechanism had become permanently activated.
- Found they're constantly on edge mentally – had a short fuse and were irritated, especially by small insignificant events.
- Found that going to school or work became difficult, often impossible to undertake.
- Became hypersensitive and inappropriately perceived almost any remark as critical;
- Became obsessed with the abusive experience that took over their lives, eclipsing and excluding almost every other interest.
- Believed that their abusive problems are hopeless and that their efforts to stop the situation will be futile.
- Been sleepless, had nightmares, constantly reliving events, woke early or woke up more tired than when they went to bed.
- Poor concentration and became forgetful especially with trivial day-to-day things.
- Experienced regular intrusive, violent visualisations and flashbacks and couldn't get the abuse out of their minds.
- Suffered from post-traumatic stress disorder (PTSD).
- Became emotional - bursting into tears regularly over trivial matters.
- Became uncharacteristically irritable, had angry outbursts, were hypersensitive and felt fragile.

- Feelings of withdrawal and isolation, wanted to be on their own and sought solitude.

The four stages of fear

Targets often go through four stages of fear when faced with anything that appears dangerous to them:

1. **Arousal** – their muscles tense, breathing and heart rate increase;
2. **Fight or Flight** – the body's automatic defence response when dealing with threat;
3. **Freezing/Immobility** – the above response is put on hold; they freeze and become unable to respond or escape from the threat;
4. **Dormant Immobility** – a rest state once the threat has passed.

Animals are generally able to return to their normal mode of functioning as soon as the danger passes, but humans often can't and may become locked into a recurring pattern of the above responses.

If the cyber bullying is threatening, children should be advised to immediately stop logging onto the site and tell their parents, a teacher, Crime Stoppers or the police.

Cyber bullying is usually not a one-time communication, unless it involves a death threat or a credible threat of serious bodily harm. In extreme cases, people have killed each other or committed suicide after being involved in a cyber bullying incident.

Children need to be reminded that if they are bullied – they're not at fault – the person doing the bullying is at fault and will be charged accordingly.

Examples of bullying

- A student is bombarded by anonymous threatening and taunting e-mails at home, even though there is no direct harassment at school.
- The target has no idea who is sending the messages and starts to feel like everybody is against him/her. That student is being cyber bullied.
- A school bulletin board is spammed with name-calling posts that spread vicious rumours about a specific student. The rumours aren't true, but kids at school see the posts and believe them. The student is then excluded by other peers. This student is the target of cyber bullying.
- A nasty fake profile is posted at a social networking site using a student's real name, photo, and contact information. That student starts getting weird e-mail messages from strangers who think the profile is real. Some of the messages are crude. Some of the messages are mean. This is another example of cyber bullying.

These are just a few examples of cyber bullying. If you are taking part in things like this – it's not harmless fun. You're being a cyber bully. If you are the target of this type of treatment you are being cyber bullied and there are things you can do to stop the harassment.

How common is cyber bullying during the teen years?

Bullying is not new but thanks to the Internet teens are now being bullied at home. On-line harassment, more often called cyber bullying, is a serious problem. When bullying comes home via the Internet it can leave targets feeling helpless and overwhelmed.

Parents should know a few cyber bullying facts before their pre-teens begin middle school. About one in five teens reports, being targeted by cyber bullying, according to a comprehensive study of nine- to eleven-year-olds. The researchers found that eleven percent of children had been targeted on-line or through their cell phones one or two times in the previous year.

An additional ten percent of the students had experienced cyber bullying three or more times in the year.

Additional cyber bullying facts: When asked about the form of the bullying, eighteen percent of the targeted teens said that the bullying happened through e-mail while seventeen percent said it occurred in a chat room. Bullying via instant messages was less common (thirteen percent), as were text messages (twelve percent), comments on a website (eleven percent), and distribution of an embarrassing photo (seven percent).

Most targeted teens said they did not know the form the cyber bullying took (twenty-five percent) or reported that it took a different form than any of the forms listed here (twenty-two percent). These findings indicate how much researchers still must learn about cyber bullying. The unclear results about forms of cyber bullying also underscore the secrecy and shame that often accompany being bullied.

Why do people cyber bully?

Some bully because their role models (often their parents or older siblings) are bullies. It's natural for children to mimic the behaviour of their role models. Others seem to be born with a lack of empathy towards others or a feeling that they're superior to others. It's almost impossible for these individuals to understand what their bullying behaviour does to their targets. Only professional counselling (sometimes lasting for years) can reverse these flawed individuals.

Bullying has been around forever, but cyber bullying is different because it lets a bully remain anonymous and thanks to the Internet, teens are now being bullied at home. It's easier to bully in cyberspace than it is to bully face to face. With cyber bullying a bully can pick on people with much less risk of being caught.

Bullies are natural instigators and in cyberspace, bullies can enlist the participation of other students who normally may not be willing to bully in the real world. Unfortunately, kids who stand around doing nothing in a bullying incident often become active participants in on-line harassment.

The detachment afforded by cyberspace makes bullies out of people who would never become involved in a real-life incident. The Internet makes bullying more convenient and since the target's reaction remains unseen, people who wouldn't normally bully don't take it as seriously.

What can be done about cyber bullying?

There are many things that can be done to combat cyber bullying.

Remember the bullies in high school when we were young? Cyber bullying is a new way to bully and crops up out of our teens' ability to connect with each other through internet social websites, e-mail and cell phones. While the ability to talk with friends in these different ways is fun, it has given bullies a new way of doing what they want to do - hurt people. And that is the main point I want to make here: Using the internet to bully is new, but bullying isn't.

Therefore, if your teen is dealing with cyber bullying, you treat it just as you would if your teen is being bullied in the school yard. Here are some tips on what you can do if your teen is dealing with cyber bullying.

Preventing cyber bullying

Teaching children to respect others and to take a stand against bullying of all kinds helps and they should be rewarded for taking that stand. Schools can work with parents to stop and remedy cyber bullying.

They can also educate the students on cyber ethics and the law. If schools are creative, they can sometimes avoid the claim that their actions exceeded their legal authority for off-campus cyber bullying actions.

Educating the kids about the consequences (losing their ISP or IM accounts) helps. Teaching them to respect others and to take a stand against bullying of all kinds helps too. Because their motives differ, the solutions and responses to each type of cyber bullying incident must differ too. Schools can work with parents to stop and remedy cyber bullying.

Often schools will enlist the help of police officers to discuss the harmful effects of cyber bullying and the penalties the bully will receive for doing so.

Parents also need to understand that a child is just as likely to be a cyber bully as a target of cyber bullying and often go back and forth between the two roles during one incident. They may not even realise that they're seen as a cyber bully.

1. **Set rules.** Parents need to make it a part of their computer rules or parenting contract that their teen will show them any threats or any type of hateful words made to them. They'll also want to stress to their teen that they will not tolerate them saying things that are hurtful to others.
2. **Teach your teen to be savvy with their social networking.** Show your teen how to delete offending messages and block cyber bullies from being able to leave messages on their social websites.
3. **Tell your teen it's okay not to 'friend' everyone** who asks on Facebook or other social network sites.

How you can stop cyber bullying once it starts:

There are two things parents must consider before anything else.

- Is their child at risk of physical harm or assault?

- How are they handling the attacks emotionally?

If there's any indication that personal contact information has been posted on-line or any threats are made to their child, they must run, not walk, to their local law enforcement agency.

Take a print-out of all instances of cyber bullying to show them, but note that a print-out is not sufficient to prove a case of cyber harassment or cyber bullying. You'll need electronic evidence and live data for that. It's crucial that all electronic evidence be preserved to allow the person to be traced and to take whatever action needs to be taken. The electronic evidence is at risk of being deleted by the Internet service providers unless you notify them immediately that you need those records preserved! So check to see which e-mail account they came in on and phone the Internet service provider.

Parents need to be the ones students trust when things go wrong on-line and/or off-line. Yet students often don't go to their parents. Why? Because their parents have a tendency to over-react. Most children will avoid telling their parents about a cyber bullying incident fearing they will only make things worse.

Unfortunately, sometimes parents also under-react. They need to be supportive of their children and realise that these attacks can follow them into their otherwise safe home and wherever they go on-line. The risk of emotional pain is very real and very serious, so parents should not ignore their plight.

Why is cyber bullying so serious?

It may seem like cyber bullying is a trivial matter. You might think the answer is to just ban them from going on-line or stop them from opening up their messages hoping everything will blow over.

Even if you believe that in-person bullying is a problem, it might seem like there's little damage that can be done on-line.

This is far from the truth, however. Cyber bullying can be even more dangerous than in-person incidents:

- It can be more difficult to stop an on-line bully.
- Emotional violence can be more damaging than physical violence.
- Cyber bullying can have long term effects as gossip, lies, photos and videos stay long after bruises fade.
- Cyber bullying follows people into the home, which would normally be considered a haven from this type of activity.
- It's easy to impersonate another person on-line, gain someone's trust and then turn on them.

Penalties for cyber bullying

Although targets might lodge criminal charges, most of the time the cyber bullying does not go so far that the law has to intervene, although targets often might attempt to lodge criminal charges. Cyber bullying however, may result in a misdemeanour cyber harassment charge, or if the bullying child is young enough may result in the charge of juvenile delinquency. It has to have a minor on both sides, or at least have been instigated by a minor against another minor for this to happen.

It typically can result in the person losing their ISP or IM accounts because s/he violated his/her terms of service rules. In some cases, if hacking or password and identity theft is involved, they can be charged with serious criminal charges by state and federal law enforcement agencies. Unfortunately, many do not report cyber bullying or don't know who to talk to about the bullying.

Because the cyber bully's motives differ, the solutions and responses to each type of cyber bullying incident has to differ as well. We encourage schools to work with parents to stop and remedy cyber bullying and educate students about cyber ethics and the law.

Deal with cyber bullying when it happens

The most important thing a target of cyber bullying can do is not respond to the bully.

- Don't play into the bully's games.
- Don't answer e-mails.
- Don't respond to posts.
- Don't engage in a chat room exchange.
- Don't copy what the bully is doing.
- Ignore the bullying and get help from parents and teachers.
- Don't ignore cyber bullying. Ever. Explain to your teen that it's not their fault they were targeted by a cyber bully. Often teens turn these problems inward and start to feel far less confident about themselves. Verbally affirm that they're not at fault and they'll be less likely to take a hit to their self-esteem level.
- Don't get involved in the cyber bulling and don't let your teen prolong it. The more you or your teen try to talk to whomever is doing the bullying, the more it will escalate and you could be found at fault for not reporting the problem in the first place.
- If your teen is cyber bullied at school, report the incident to the school. Include a screen shot or copy of the e-mail where the cyber bullying took place. If the school is unable to do anything, report the incident to the police.
- Also, be sure to report the incident to your internet service. If the cyber bullying incident takes place while your teen is at home, report the incident to the ISP of the offender by forwarding the e-mail or reporting it to the site it occurred on.

- If the cyber bullying includes threats of physical violence, report them to your local police ***immediately***. This may seem harsh, because it's an e-mail and the person is not right there now, but a physical threat of violence is nothing to take lightly. Protect your teen. You should especially report it to the police if it continues for any length in time and is not just a one-time incident.
- If the cyber bullying is happening anonymously, ***it's even more important to report it.*** It may never turn into something violent, but many times it does. The police can track down who's sending the e-mails - so let them handle it.
- While you will ignore the bully, be sure to save the evidence, so that school officials, Internet providers and even the police can properly deal with the bully. Cyber bullying may give bullies anonymity but it always leaves evidence and a trail of information that can be checked out by experts.

Why is cyber bullying so difficult to stop?

- Traditional bullies might be suspended from school, banned from certain places or activities or even arrested, but cyber bullies are more elusive.
- The anonymity of the Internet makes it difficult to be sure who's doing the bullying.
- The anonymity of the Internet makes cyber bullies (especially kids) bolder.
- Cyber bullying can cross state and even international lines, making it nearly impossible for victims to prosecute the culprits.
- Most cyber bullies may think they won't get caught or punished.
- Others may play down the damage the cyber bully is doing.

Can cyber bullying be stopped?

Schools must take all types of bullying seriously. As soon as the cyber bullying starts, go to school officials for help. Ask to see their policy about bullying and cyber bullying because cyber bullying is often an extension or escalation of bullying that's already happening at school. If this is the case, ask what has been done to stop the bullying. Parents should be kept informed about what's happening now and what has happened in the past.

The police are unlikely to become involved if the bullying is limited to a few isolated incidents or a couple of mean e-mails or instant messages. However, if you get even one communication that includes a threat of bodily harm or a death threat the police should be alerted immediately.

About twenty youths across Queensland take their lives each year. Most are between fifteen and seventeen years-of-age, but suicides of children aged ten to fourteen have increased. Content on on-line forums such as Facebook and Tumblr heighten the risk of copycat suicides where users urge others to take their own lives or harm themselves.

Be aware that others urging people to commit suicide is considered a death threat and the police will treat it accordingly.

Vulnerable children who've been bullied or have mental health issues are at risk. Parents need to carefully monitor what happens to them on social media or texting on their phones.

When should the police become involved?

Repeated or excessive harassment via e-mail, forums or chat rooms is harassment and should involve the police. Threats of violence should be reported to the police. Be sure to save all messages as evidence. The police will know what to do with them.

Don't put up with cyber bullying; get help. Cyber bullying leaves a clear trail of evidence and this can work to the advantage of the target. Cyber bullies are just bullies with a new weapon in their arsenal of harassment, so treat them like you would any bully and they lose their power.

How to prevent your child from being targeted

Be your child's support system.

The biggest way to prevent your child from being a target is to keep the lines of communication open. This means walking a fine line between a concerned caregiver and an overprotective parent. Your child needs to feel that s/he can come to you without negative repercussions. If they're afraid you'll ban them from using the Internet or keep them from going out with friends, they will not confide in you. It also means listening carefully and avoiding the tendency to trivialise what they're experiencing. It may not seem like a big deal to an adult that the most popular kids in school made fun of your child's hair or clothes, but it can be a serious blow to the self-esteem of a child or teen if that happens.

Be firm.

Set rules regarding when and how long your child can be on-line. Accessing the Internet is akin to inviting someone into your home, so you may choose to only allow Web time when you're at home. Use Internet filters, timers, and whatever else you need to do to protect your child.

Know your child.

This is very important. Kids who are already suffering from low self-esteem or depression are prime targets for cyber bullying. It can be tempting to assume that your child is just going through a phase or that they're just in a 'bad mood,' but you're better off seeking professional help if there's a problem rather than simply waiting things out.

Know the danger signs.

Your child may become more withdrawn or moody. S/he may spend more time on-line, or may refuse to use the computer altogether. They may cut off ties with friends. If your child gives any indication that they are being bullied on or off-line, take it seriously.

Educate.

Teach your child what to do in cases where they feel threatened or bullied. They should ignore the offender and contact an adult immediately. They should never engage with the person who's threatening them as that will only encourage the behaviour to continue. As an adult, if you feel threatened by someone on-line, contact the police just to be safe. You can also use built-in measures on certain websites, such as ignoring or reporting someone else.

Chapter 11
WORKPLACE BULLYING

Workplace bullying is the deliberate, repeated and hurtful mistreatment of one person by another. Others refer to it as harassment, emotional abuse, targeted aggression or abuse of power that undermines self-confidence and causes stress. It's constant, inappropriate, overt and covert behaviour that criticises, belittles, isolates and undermines the victim. It involves humiliation, sabotage, spreading gossip, overwork, unnecessary pressure, delaying tactics and it can escalate into physical and verbal assault, sexual assault and arson. Evidence shows that bullying is normally repeated and can escalate in intensity over time.

Have you ever wondered how the bullies you saw at school are now? Chances are they're still making someone's life hell, but this time, in the workplace. An employee's worst nightmare may be that one of them might be their direct supervisor. It almost seems that those young sandbox bullies (male and female) grow up, trade in their cute little shorts for fancy business suits and a slick hairdo and continue to apply their bullying behaviour to ensure their career success.

New studies indicate that childhood bullying leads to workplace bullying, that children who are victims of school bullies, often become victims as adults. Bullies themselves also tend to be unpopular, both in schools and later in the workplace. They maintain relationships (not friendships) by displays of strength and by inducing fear to gain respect.

Cultural influences may play a part in bullying. Some women feel powerless when relating to men, which may prevent women from taking action to stop the bullying. Others have been brought up to respect their elders and people in authority. As a result, they may find it difficult to confront bullying if perpetrated by an older person or authority figure.

Workplace bullying is not limited to bosses. It can come from peers, especially those who are jealous or are threatened by their colleague's abilities and/or success. Finally, workplace bullies are differentiated by gender. Women can be equally as vicious as men in spite of using more verbal techniques.

Should their target assert his/her right not to be bullied, a paranoid fear of exposure compels the bully to perceive that person as a threat and hence neutralise and dispose of him/her as quickly as possible. Once that person has been eliminated, there's an interval before the bully chooses another target and the cycle begins again.

Guidelines issued by the Commonwealth Public Service Commission describe workplace harassment as a form of employment discrimination, consisting of offensive, abusive, belittling or threatening behaviour directed at an individual worker or group of workers which may be a result of some real or perceived attribute or difference. However, these ***Guidelines*** are not backed up by specific laws.

The workplace epidemic:

Bullying is spreading through the workplace like an epidemic. Whereas twenty years ago most people could reasonably have expected to go through their working life without a serious bullying incident, today almost everyone seems to be at risk of being severely bullied during their career, maybe more than once.

Bullies torment, browbeat and harass others to hide their weaknesses and inadequacy and to divert attention away from their incompetence. If employers took the time to determine the cost of high sick leave, staff turnover, low employee morale, poor productivity and customer service they would realise the cost of allowing bullying to continue in their workplaces is counter-productive.

Because workplace bullying doesn't always leave physical evidence, it's not well documented and since it rarely erupts into open confrontation, it's also the most tolerated of all workplace behaviour. Verbally harassed workers don't express their feelings, fearing what they reveal will be used by their tormentors to 'prove' their instability. Many employees who speak up are isolated and suffer greater harassment or their co-workers erect a wall of silence. Some insist the episode didn't happen the way it did. For all harassed workers, a tight job market adds to the dilemma, so they adapt - try to handle it - and just cope. But the diminished self-esteem, the energy that's consumed day after day going back to that kind of emotional beating, takes its toll.

If enough people do not defend the victim - the person begins to believe they're crazy, feel guilty or that they could be magnifying the situation. Victims also fear retaliation, ridicule and harassment if they complain. On-the-job harassment could be compared to the battered wife syndrome: the emotional effects are the same. There are parallels between family violence and violence against women in the workplace, including the fact that in both cases violence usually represents an abuse of power.

Most employers have distinguished themselves by their inaction - even when bullying has been reported. In a competitive business environment where profit often takes precedence over personnel, self-monitoring may be insufficient.

Some describe their office as toxic because of the toll they take causing stressed, overworked employees to become sick or to leave the company. Turnover in many companies has risen to epidemic proportions. Many companies are downsizing or merging with other companies who use different styles of leadership. After a takeover, this can lead to a loss of up to 75 per cent in work productivity. Or companies promote managers who may have high technical knowledge, but their people-skills must have been taught at the Saddam Hussein School of business.

Cost to companies:

Bullying in the workplace has proven to be one of the most costly disciplinary matters a company can deal with. If not dealt with swiftly and aggressively, it can result in loss of productivity and de-motivation of any staff that have either observed or been subjected to the bullying. It can cause high absenteeism, loss of job satisfaction and often involves the loss of good employees who will not tolerate such seemingly condoned behaviour by their companies.

Hidden direct costs include those associated with pursuing formal grievance procedures, other staff time in addressing bullying-related incidents and workers' compensation costs. Lost productivity costs include not only those costs arising from reduced performance by victims while at work, but also lower initial efficiency among replacement employees until they reach the same level of performance as those replaced.

This also can apply if the victim or bully is transferred to a new position within the organisation. It also includes productivity loss among co-workers who are affected by the bullying. Then there are the consequences of bullying and its stress as it impacts on worker innovation and creativity. There may also be detrimental effects on company image where the organisation is involved in a highly publicised case, with resultant impact on shareholders.

If the employee leaves in disgust because of inaction by the company to deal with the bullying issue, they might find that the company gives them a bad or no reference. If they pursue the issue and take the harassment and victimisation charges to court - they will likely need a big purse to cover the cost of the legal expenses. Most don't bother and go on to better things and the bullies win again.

There are many consequences for organisations. They include direct economic impacts such as the costs of paid sick leave, replacing staff and the legal and compensation costs arising from complaints and grievances. Absenteeism and staff turnover rates have been reported at very high rates in some overseas studies, up to 87 per cent absenteeism and 82 per cent staff turnover.

Workplace bullying has serious economic effects on Australian organisations. In one Australian study 34 per cent of bullied victims took time off work. The average time taken was 50 days, including 28 days on paid sick leave. Almost one-quarter resigned or retired and organisations incur costs in replacing those staff as well as losing valuable experience.

A recent impact and cost assessment calculated that workplace bullying costs Australian employers between $6 and $13 billion dollars every year when hidden and lost opportunity costs are considered and when using a very conservative prevalence estimate of the extent of overall victimisation and up to $17 and $36 billion per year when a somewhat higher estimate of 15 per cent prevalence is applied.

Serious bullying costs an average of $17,000 per case, but most Australian managers don't realise the cost of bullying, so pretend it isn't happening in their businesses. My research has identified that the majority of supervisors in Australia have not received even basic supervisory training so are blundering their way in business and making costly mistakes.

Most managers view people who complain of bullying as sissies or poor team members who don't play by the rules to meet performance measures. Some people just expect to get pushed around and others expect they will be able to push other people around. People being bullied often resign from their jobs instead of reporting the bullying, which hides the problem even more. The victims fear they won't be believed or that they will get a bad reference if they 'make waves.' So they simply leave and go elsewhere. This is why businesses should conduct exit interviews to determine the reasons why their employees leave their company. Many companies, instead of censuring the bully, transfer him or her to another department and the cycle continues in the new department.

New attitudes towards supervision:

Until recently, psychologically violent people in the workplace were regarded as tough managers or difficult people or at worst a 'pain in the neck.' These attitudes are changing as the dysfunction, inefficiency, cost and severe psychiatric injury they inflict on others is revealed. The serial bully in the workplace is often found in a job that is a position of power, has a high administrative or procedural content, but little or no creative requirement which provides opportunities for demonstrating a caring or leadership nature.

Many managers fear the stigma of being branded a bully and then having to defend such allegations in a stress claim. An employer or manager has the right to instruct an employee on how the work is to be done in the workplace, but are not allowed to carry it to the level where it could be considered bullying. Many find that the blurring of the line between performance management and harassment has made it harder for managers to manage.

Workplace harassment may be distinguished from legitimate comments on the work performance of a subordinate employee by his or her supervisor. It's acceptable and indeed good management practice requires, that supervisors inform their subordinates of what is expected of them, the extent to which they meet those expectations and where they do not and what can be done to overcome perceived problems. It is not workplace harassment for managers to manage.

So how do managers decide when that line has been crossed and what does bullying behaviour look like? Typically, it comes from a boss to a subordinate in the form of verbal or emotional abuse. It includes yelling, swearing or ridiculing, continual and trivial fault-finding, chronic unjustified criticism, berating, intimidation, public humiliation or sabotaging of achievements. But the workplace bully can also be the silent snake-in-the-grass who cruelly bullies through manipulation, isolation, exclusion and gossip. Or they set an employee up to fail by overloading them with work, inconsistently and unjustifiably changing work responsibilities and even cancelling scheduled holidays.

What do the experts have to say?

So, how do you deal with a person who is a compulsive liar with a Jekyll and Hyde nature, is charming and glib, excels at deception and evasion of accountability? Diagnosis of such an individual is challenging. This is especially difficult should that person's superiors behave in a similar manner, give him or her glowing reports and deny everything. Let's see what the experts have to say:

Adelaide-based **Working Women's Centre** director, Sandra Dann said the extent of bullying uncovered was 'pretty horrifying.' She described the practice as 'highly entrenched,' in large organisations with a hierarchical management approach. She said bullying was a 'symptom of a sick workplace - not of gender,' noting male bullying was more likely to have violent or sexual undertones. She denies the number of women bullies was increasing, saying they were just more identifiable. But whoever the perpetrator, the cost to society is significant. The WWC survey found more than half of respondents reported the incidents to their managers, but did not receive adequate support or help. She says, *'Knowing there are penalties if you break the law, is a good incentive to start doing the right thing by workers.'* She also called for 'accessible' legal redress for victims.

Lack of Workplace Bullying protection in Australia:

The following **Occupational Health and Safety** regulations were updated as follows:

- South Australia: 1972 and 1984-1987

- Tasmania: 1977 and 1995
- Victoria: 1981 and 1986
- New South Wales: 1983 and 2000
- Northern Territory: 1984-1987
- Western Australia: 1989
- Queensland: 1995
- Australian Capital Territory: 1991 (Commonwealth employees)
- Australian Capital Territory: 1993 (Maritime industry)

[**Note:** I did a spell-check on these regulations and found that none of the Occupational Health and Safety regulations in Australia cover workplace bullying, harassment or violence in the workplace] although most progressive countries do.

An Australia-wide survey conducted by the ***Morgan & Banks*** recruitment firm shows more than 10 per cent of respondents report bullying is increasing at work. At least half the cost of work-associated stress is directly attributable to bullying.

The ***North West Adelaide Health Service*** alone loses about $5 million a year in bullying-related costs. A new program aims to cut that figure in half.

Drake Personnel chief Diane Utatao said that workplace bullying affects one-in-four Australians and costs employers up to $12 billion a year and that the antics of one serial bully had the potential to reduce the performance of his/her victim in half and that of other employees by up to 33 per cent. Because the bully is bullying, they too are a productivity drain. She said that permanent employees in fear of losing their jobs were more likely to put up with bullying.

When a worker tries to attribute the injury to workplace bullying, workers compensation more often than not reject the claim (unconfirmed reports claim 95% of all stress-leave claims are initially rejected) by WorkCover insurance companies. In the meantime, the victim and bully often continue to work together - and the bullying may continue. Because of this, many workers are forced to go on stress leave, rather than continue to work in the same vicinity as their bully. Unless the company deals with and settles the issue within a short period of time - the victim's stress level can increase - rather than be alleviated. The longer the process takes to be resolved, the more chance that the victim will resign or go on stress leave. And the bully will likely go unpunished.

Claims that are accepted by WorkCover may take six to nine months to process. All that time, the bullying could be continuing or the claimant could be away from work on stress leave. Mediation is often recommended but mediation involves the victim and the offender facing each other. Mediation can be so distressing for some victims that it's cruel. Bullies can be very persuasive and end up making the victim feel bullied during the mediation. It might be necessary to bring the bully to account more directly under the enterprise bargaining agreement or their employment contract.

Young doctors were found to be falsifying work records, dropping out of their specialist courses or abandoning their medical profession. Although bullying is of epidemic proportions, many accept it as a rite of passage to become doctors. Some see it as survival of the strongest. Senior specialists are bullying juniors to a point that some suffer from depression and may have thoughts of or attempt suicide. This entrenched culture of medical bullies is diverting millions of dollars from the cash-strapped public health system by sick leave and lost productivity. Surveys found that 10 per cent of staff felt bullied, but new training programs and complaint systems aim to slash the problem.

And there's trouble in our courts and legislative assemblies too. As **Queensland District Court, J. Dodds** states, *'In today's Australian community it is not acceptable (if ever it* was) *for a person in authority over another in a workplace to harass, belittle or demean that other as a method of enforcing his authority or relieving his frustration.'*

Unfortunately in our legislative assemblies bullying is a way of life that sets a dangerous precedent for the rest of business society. For too long, strong leadership in politics and in the corporate sector has been equated with table-thumping, shouting and dressing-down - especially in parliamentary debates. Politicians need to look closer to home when setting laws for their states and ensure they abide by them as well!

A **TMP Worldwide Survey on Bullying** said that of the 5,000 Australian employees questioned, 18 per cent said their boss bullied them and their co-workers, with 29 per cent reporting that employers are more hostile towards their employees than they were ten years ago. The survey shows that the biggest bullying bosses emanate from the legal sector with a massive 33.3 per cent of respondents in that industry saying they were experiencing bullying tactics from their employers. Government sector bosses were not that far behind in the bullying stakes with 21.6 per cent of personnel in that sector saying their bosses were bullies.

Mr. Geoff Qurban of TMP Worldwide says, *'Times get tough, sometimes the tough get going and forget about the niceties and good manners expected of them in the workplace.'*

'A downturn in the economy always brings about the worst in bosses' interpersonal skills. The pressure is on them to make the bottom line look good. They need to make sure that everyone in their operation is pulling their weight and they probably are at the brunt of external factors too, like looking for new markets, developing new products and maintaining a financial even keel.'

'Most employees, i.e. 34.8 per cent, said the number one factor that makes their bosses belligerent is the inability to communicate and only 34.8 per cent said it was the pressure

to produce. 12.9 per cent of respondents said it was their bosses inexperience to cope with the job and 11.25 per cent said it was the difficulty in obtaining a good work/life balance that made their boss belligerent.'

Workplace stress management:

There are many areas where managers can work to reduce stress in order to create a workplace environment where there is higher productivity and fewer stress-related claims, sick days and accidents. To do this, managers should:

- Identify all the possible causes of stress.
- Eliminate harassment in the workplace. Conduct an assessment of all areas of workplace life that could contribute to stress. Determine the frequency and duration of stressors and the health impact on employees.
- Find ways of controlling stress levels by modifying the workplace, work systems or management style.

This process should be on-going. Frustration through lack of control can lead to a steady build-up of stress. Those who rate their jobs as demanding, but who have little control, are more likely to suffer from workplace stress. A WorkCover claim for stress should be managed in the same way as all other occupational injury or illness. *Unfortunately most claims for occupational stress are initially disputed by the insurance company.* Those who have been subject to workplace harassment and have been forced to take stress leave will have to be diligent in their efforts to prove their case.

Griffith University Workplace Bulling and Violence Project Team's information sheet on workplace bullying states that there has been no Australian research surveying the general population or large representative employee groups, so that we do not yet have reliable statistics on the number of Australians experiencing workplace bullying.

The best international research shows between 25 and 50 per cent of employees will experience bullying at some time in their working lives (although in some occupations, the figure is up to 95 per cent) and 4 to 20 per cent of people have been bullied in the past six to twelve months. Best estimates based on international research extrapolated to the Australian population is that 10 to 15 per cent of the Australian labour force will experience workplace bullying in a given year. This means about one million Australians have experienced the direct effects of workplace bullying during the past twelve months and about five million Australians will have experienced it at some point during their working lives.

Recent research shows that workplace bullying affects not only those directly victimised, but also other workers who witness bullying incidents as well as the families of victims. Therefore, a much larger number of Australians are affected each year by the consequences of workplace bullying than the actual number of victims.

Implementing an anti-bullying policy:

An anti-bullying policy can be implemented with minimal cost within an organisation's existing anti-harassment, equity and conflict resolution procedures. As such, it offers a cost-effective way of minimising risks of the costly impact of bullying.

Implementation of the policy sends a positive message to staff, clients, investors and other key stakeholders that negative behaviours that disrupt productivity and quality and undermine customer service will not be tolerated. In these terms an anti-bullying policy signals that the organisation is responsible and ethical and cares about maintaining motivated committed staff and good customer relations.

Recommendations:

Here's a summary of my findings and recommendations to overcome workplace bullying, harassment and violence in the workplace:

Finding: Most government departments responsible for the safety and well-being of employees fail to protect workers from workplace bullying, harassment and violence. Many governmental departments have spent a fortune on task forces to upgrade their regulations relating to workplace bullying, but have ignored the findings of these groups. Instead of changing the legislation to state in fact, "thou shalt not," and give the consequences should companies break those regulations, many have released *"Guidence"* notes to businesses. Remember that: *Regulations have the force of law, whereas "Codes of Conduct" and "Guidance Notes" contain only guidance material* so they can be and are mainly ignored.

Recommendation: Review the findings of the taskforces and implement the changes they've recommended. Make them law - rather than leave it up to the discretion of individual companies to do the right thing. Have regular training sessions where government representatives make sure that supervisors and managers know their responsibilities relating to violence, bullying and harassment and back these up with the regulations in the acts that state these. I know training is done now, but most are not backed up by government regulations with "teeth."

Forget about sending *"Guidance"* notes to businesses (unless they're just information on how to implement the government regulations shown in the different Acts). Send them copies of the legislated regulations and make sure they abide by them. Canberra should be setting an example and all laws related to Work-place Health & Safety, Occupational Health & Safety, Human Rights & Equal Opportunity, Anti-Discrimination and

WorkCover should be the same across Australia. It shouldn't matter where an employee lives - the laws concerning violence, bullying and harassment should be the same. And the consequences to companies should be fast and effective.

Finding: Companies are not forced to post Zero-Tolerance Harassment and Bullying policies (should be made law) for their companies to see. Many companies see bullying as a way of doing business and they won't change unless forced to do so by government regulations. No amount of *"Guidance Notes"* will do this.

Recommendation: Companies must learn (through television if necessary) that workplace bullying is simply not acceptable. There have been a few stabs at doing this (which were well done) but it's simply not enough. Businesses need to be reminded that well-run companies <u>always</u> have clear policies and procedures (available to all employees) relating to human resource issues (such as bullying, discipline, written warnings, grievance procedures, sexual harassment, WorkCover, equal employment etc.) and that they are enforced.

Routinely, candidates that apply for positions should ask potential companies, *"Does your company have written policies and procedures relating to workplace bullying and harassment?"*

Only then, will some companies realise that they should have them in place. If they don't have them in place, the employee will know that his or her chances are slim that these companies will deal effectively with bullying episodes.

Finding: If companies don't deal effectively with bullying incidents, discipline the bullies and stop the unacceptable behaviour, employees will continue to have no other options but to quit their jobs or take their bullies (and the companies they work for) to court. This long and drawn-out process can take anywhere from two to five years to accomplish. Not only does it take a long time, but it can cost the employee tens of thousands of dollars in legal costs (often $50 - $100,000). In many cases, settlement does not even cover the legal expenses and *fines do not go to the victim*. Most come away feeling like they've been "had" and that the company (that defended the bully) appear to have condoned that despicable behaviour. In the interim, the victims may have to work side-by-side with his or her bully until his or her allegations are dealt with.

Recommendation: Bullying will continue, unless governments get off their duffs and legislate regulations that have some teeth in them relating to workplace bullying, harassment and violence. These government departments should be protecting the workers and supplying the legal assistance to the bullied employees. Employees should not have to bear the costs to legally stop their bully. Court fines of the companies should pay for the employees' legal fees.

Finding: If the employees are so stressed that they must go on stress leave while they wait for the bullying charges to be dealt with, they may or may not receive payment for that stress leave from their employer's WorkCover insurance company. Unfortunately victims often won't know that the payment will not be paid until three or four months into the stress leave - causing more financial grief to the victims. WorkCover insurance companies need to be monitored to ensure that this does not happen.

Recommendation: These WorkCover insurance companies must investigate every stress leave claim lodged by bullied employees with an open mind. They need to be able to see the issue from the employee's point of view and assume that the victim is indeed in dire need of their stress leave. I can only assume that because the company the employee is working for pays for the WorkCover, that the insurance company sees the issue only from the company's point of view.

Although WorkCover insurance companies state that they cover stress leave, I have unconfirmed reports that even with proper medical documentation, most of them automatically reject 95 per cent of all claims. Therefore employees are forced to fight WorkCover insurers to obtain the money they should rightly receive. The last thing these stressed-out bullied people need is another battle to fight - but often that's exactly what happens! Many give up – they're too worn down to keep fighting.

Finding: The phenomenal cost of workplace bullying must stop. It's not only the employee who pays by going through the trauma, but companies pay dearly through loss of productivity of the victim and surrounding staff, payment for stress leave and having to replace either the bully or the victim (who often leaves in disgust). And how about the witnesses to the bullying? This results in lowered morale, they become less motivated to do a good job and become disgusted themselves when they observe that nothing is done to correct the bullying behaviour. They wonder *"Will I be next? What or who will protect me if the bully starts picking on me."*

Recommendation: Australian industry must be made aware of the horrific costs of workplace bullying. 1,100 Victorian claims for compensation as a result of workplace violence, harassment and bullying cost $26 million. Bullying costs the Australian economy up to $13 billion a year in absenteeism, compensation, management time and lost productivity - and these are not the most recent figures. With approximately 24.292 million population in Australia that means that companies stand to lose an average of $653.25 per person per year due to bullying and its after-effects. Not good for Australian business or the GNP!

Finding: Some bullied employees never recover from the trauma. Self-esteem plummets and stress levels rise. This can cripple the most assertive individual.

Recommendation: The only resolution to this is to stop bullying behaviour in its tracks. This can only occur with:

- The support of proper government legislation to deal with workplace bullying, harassment and violence.
- Monitoring to see that companies follow the regulations;
- Giving support to the "little guy" (the employee).
- A complete changeover from the macho, draconian way of supervision that's part of the Australian business culture.

Finding: If co-workers don't rally behind the victim, the target can suffer additional emotional trauma of having to go through the ordeal alone.

Recommendation: Many victims I spoke with were as traumatised by the lack of support they received from people who witnessed the bullying. Their faith in their fellow man was shattered (in some cases never to be restored) because their fellow workers refused to corroborate their information. *Witnesses to bullying behaviour must speak up - shame on them for not doing so.* I don't know how they can look themselves in the mirror every day - how they could even contemplate letting down a co-worker. The truth is the truth and witnesses should get some backbone and defend the victim - because who knows - they may be the bully's next target.

No longer should a person be ridiculed because s/he dobbed in a bully. Nor should it be acceptable for observers to stand by and not get involved in supporting the victim.

Finding: Families suffer due to the victim's agitation and stress. Spouses feel helpless as they watch their loved ones dwindle in stature before their eyes. The often carefree individual - suddenly can't function. The job they once loved, now involves a daily struggle to get up and go into work.

Recommendation: Until the victims receive the support they need from all avenues, these families will continue to suffer. Companies should be encouraged to have Employee Assistance Programs that provide free psychological treatment for employees facing trauma.

Finding: Although Australian corporations preach that they advocate that their employees should maintain a good work/life balance, many are literally working their employees to death. Stress levels are at all-time highs with no end in sight.

Recommendation: Laws must be enforced that protect workers from overwork with statutes such as:

- Hours of work must be confined within a period of 12 consecutive hours in any one day.
- If an employee works 44 hours or less in a one week period, but works more than 8 hours in any day, overtime shall be paid for each hour in excess of 8 hours per day.
- If an employee works more than 44 hours in a one-week period, the hours of work in excess of 8 hours in each day shall be totalled and the hours of work in excess of 44 hours in a week shall be calculated. The overtime rate shall be paid for whichever is greater. Employees must receive no less than one and one-half times their regular wage for overtime pay.
- If requested, instead of overtime pay, employees can receive time off with regular pay equal to the number of overtime hours worked.
- All employees who are not exempt are paid overtime pay. Exempt employees are supervisors or managerial staff - confidential in nature. If the person is a "working supervisor" or lead hand, who in addition to supervising staff, do essentially the same work as his/her staff; they are *not* exempt and should be paid overtime.

Finding: Many victims who leave the company without a proper resolution (and some even with one) are not able to obtain a proper reference from the bullying company. The target's faith in their ability to continue in their chosen field or to even do their job plummets and many spend months being unemployed. Often they must seek psychiatric help to get their feet back on the road to recovery.

Recommendation: In the ideal world, the regulatory bodies would be the ones taking the company to court and the employee would be supported both financially and emotionally through the process. Fines should be paid to the bully – not put back into a fund or the court's pockets.

After it's been proven that bullying took place and the employee has left the company - part of the settlement would be that the company must give a favourable reference. I know of one company that simply refused to give *any* kind of reference - leaving the receiver of the information wondering why the person left the company. No reference - is as damaging as a bad reference.

Conclusion:

As I conducted research for this chapter I found myself becoming more and more depressed at the way the world deals with workplace bullying, harassment and violence. As an Australian, I became more and more disgusted with the lack of governmental action to stop it. We are not a third world country, yet we treat some of our people in the most appalling way! Australia should be ashamed of this governmental and corporate disgrace! Employees *must* be protected and unless governments become proactive - *this will not happen*.

The bottom line is that *"Codes of Practice"* and *"Guidance Notes"* are useless unless legislation (Acts relating to workplace bullying, harassment and violence) have regulations with some teeth. Occupational Health and Safety regulations appear to be the most logical Acts to include this coverage.

Australian society needs to look seriously at cleaning up the violence we now see in several of our sports. Sport used to be "sportsmanlike" but the violent actions we see in our football players can not be called sporting at all. The AFL and Aussie Rules administratiuon staff should look at the image they are giving to young Australian supporters. This is ***not*** sportsmanship – ***it's bullying*** and sets a terrible example for the impressionable youngsters of Australia. They should be ashamed of themselves!

If you're being bullied in the workplace 'Just say NO' and complain to upper management. If they don't do anything to alleviate the situation – leave your position and try to find a workplace that won't tolerate workplace harassment, bullying or violence.

In the meantime, lobby your federal and state representatives to encourage them to implement zero-tolerance workplace bullying **laws** so workers are protected against such unacceptable behaviour.

CONCLUSION

As we all go through life we're faced with making many tough decisions on what to do when faced with what could possibly be life-changing decisions. In this book we have discussed:

- how to say 'No' to using synthetic or illegal drugs like ICE (methamphetamine), heroin or cocaine.
- whether you should contemplate having pre-marital sex;
- how to say 'No' to a persistent lover who wants sex;
- date rape and stalking;
- pornography;
- how to leave a domestic violence situation;
- how to report that an adult has mentally, physically or sexually abused a child;
- how a child can report being abused;
- how to deal with elder abuse
- why social media is so dangerous;
- how to deal with school bullying;
- how to deal with cyber bullying:
- how to deal with workplace bullying;

Life is not easy, but many seem to make it through this minefield and live happy productive lives by 'Just saying NO.'

WEB CONNECTIONS

Smoke Gets in your Eyes - Elaine Hollingsworth
www.doctorsaredangerous.com

Resources for parents and kids:

www.notforkids.info is a book for younger children to teach them how to respond if they see images online that make them feel uncomfortable.

www.itstimewetalked.com.au has fact sheets about how to start a conversation about pornography and the damage it can do.

Resources for Elder Abuse:

Elder Abuse Helpline
www.eapu.com.au/Welcome.aspx for free and confidential advice for anyone experiencing elder abuse or who suspects someone they know may be experiencing elder abuse.

Legal support for seniors
www.qld.gov.au/seniors/legal-finance-concessions/legal-services

Office of the Public Guardian looks after the interests of adults with impaired capacity.
www.publicguardian.qld.gov.au/adult-guardian

Resources for synthetic and illegal drugs:

Crime Stoppers Queensland - New Synthetic Drugs: Real Damage - Doctor Interview
https://www.youtube.com/watch?v=xp0_aWr77t4

© *Australian Drug Foundation 2014.* Used with permission - See more at:
www.adf.org.au/legal-miscellaneous/australian-drug-foundation-copyright-requests#sthashZAdBXstZ.dpuf

www.ingramcontent.com/pod-product-compliance
Lightning Source LLC
LaVergne TN
LVHW051519070426
835507LV00023B/3193